THE
SPIRITUAL
WARRIOR'S
PRAYER GUIDE

QUIN SHERRER
RUTHANNE GARLOCK

Regal

From Gospel Light
Ventura, California, U.S.A.

D0067162

Published by Regal
From Gospel Light
Ventura, California, U.S.A.
www.regalbooks.com
Printed in the U.S.A.

First edition published by Servant Publications in 1992.
Second edition published by Regal Books in 2010.

Library of Congress Cataloging-in-Publication Data
The Library of Congress has catalogued the first edition as follows:
Sherrer, Quin
The spiritual warrior's prayer guide / Quin Sherrer and Ruthanne Garlock.
p. cm.
Includes bibliographical references.
ISBN 9780830747122
1. Spiritual warfare—Prayer-books and devotions—English. I. Garlock, Ruthanne. II. Title.
BV4509.5.S47 1992
248.3'2—dc20
92-22920

1 2 3 4 5 6 7 8 9 10 / 16 15 14 13 12 11 10

Rights for publishing this book outside the U.S.A. or in non-English languages are
administered by Gospel Light Worldwide, an international not-for-profit ministry.
For additional information, please visit www.glww.org, email info@glww.org, or write to
Gospel Light Worldwide, 1957 Eastman Avenue, Ventura, CA 93003, U.S.A.

With great appreciation,
we dedicate this book:

To our family members and prayer partners who
have faithfully prayed with us over the years . . .

To the new generation of warriors now taking
their place in the battle . . .

And to Jesus, our Mighty Warrior,
who leads us into triumph.

CONTENTS

PART IV: STANDING IN THE GAP

FOREWORD

Recently, I heard a prophetic word in which the Lord said, "Quit complaining about all the shaking, for this shaking is an answer to your prayers!"

This word challenged my perspective on all that is occurring in the earth today, but I had to embrace the message, as I was the one who had given it! What we see happening is not an economic crisis, nor a political crisis, but rather a spiritual crisis. I believe everything that can be shaken is being shaken so that only that which cannot be shaken will remain (see Hebrews 12:26-29).

This is evidence that the prayers of the saints of God are prevailing as a spiritual battle rages over nations and generations. Despite corporate failures, personal bankruptcies, political uncertainty, corruption in governments, natural disasters and moral decline, God is awakening His people to the power and authority given to us through His Word to bring change.

As God's change agents in the earth, we must recognize that if things are going to shift in our families, cities and even nations, we are the ones God is anointing to implement such a shift. But this will only happen as we use strategic spiritual weapons through prayer, adopting an aggressive stance of dominion grounded in the mandate found in Scripture.

My family experienced this truth years ago when we relocated our ministry, Christian International, to a region in the Florida panhandle that was saturated with a spirit of witchcraft and poverty. Within a 10-mile radius of our property there were 10 identifiable cult groups, including Satanists, Santeria, witch's covens, psychic healers and New Age gurus. It was as though God had dropped this little pioneering prophetic ministry into a land overrun by demonic forces and said, "fight or die."

At the time, there wasn't much teaching regarding spiritual warfare, so we searched the Word of God as the source of our victory and did on-the-job training to learn how to shift the spiritual atmosphere over our land. These evil strongholds resented our presence, but we were determined to push back the gates of hell and to create an open heaven over our area that would result in transformation for the glory of God's kingdom. Through persistent prayer, aggressive praise and prophetic decrees, we began to see these cultic groups shut down or relocate to other areas. When they left, so did the spirit of poverty. God has brought change to this region because a group of believers determined to exercise the authority of Scripture through spiritual warfare to see it come forth.

That is why I am so grateful for my friends Quin Sherrer and Ruthanne Garlock, who had the foresight to create a manual to train prayer warriors for effective battle through using the power of God's Word. The book you now hold in your hands, *The Spiritual Warrior's Prayer Guide*, is a powerful and relevant tool for believers to maximize their spiritual potential to be change agents in the earth.

Whether you are just learning to pray for breakthrough for your family or personal situation or you are executing spiritual assignments to pray for change in cities and nations, this guide will equip you through the Word of God. It will enlighten you with strategies to achieve victory over every evil force.

Quin and Ruthanne are two spiritual generals who have empowered a generation to contend with the powers of darkness to see people set free, circumstances shift and territories transformed for the expansion of God's kingdom. I highly recommend that each believer not only read this book but also keep it handy as a reference for all future spiritual battles.

Jane Hamon, Co-pastor
Christian International
Santa Rosa Beach, Florida

My word that goes out from my mouth:
It will not return to me empty,
but will accomplish what I desire
and achieve the purpose for which I sent it.

ISAIAH 55:11

INTRODUCTION

The apostle Paul challenges believers to oppose the powers of darkness while standing in God's strength and armor, and to "pray in the Spirit on all occasions with all kinds of prayers" (Ephesians 6:18). We cannot afford to remain passive in the face of these foes. Here are just a few examples of the many readers who have written us asking for help in spiritual warfare. As you can see, some feel almost overwhelmed by these powers of darkness:

- A mother requests prayer ammunition to fight for the deliverance of her 16-year-old son, who has been dabbling in the occult and been diagnosed as manic-depressive.

- A pastor is concerned that Satan has so blinded believers that most are living spiritually unproductive lives.

- An immigrant from Europe wants to find a church that believes in prayer and spiritual warfare. "I have no friend or prayer partner to help me," he says.

- A teenager wants to follow Jesus, but she is struggling. "I'm beginning to understand what kind of a war we really are in," she says. "Satan tries to confuse me and blind me, and tells me I'll fall back into my old routine."

- A young woman who was sexually abused by her stepfather (a pastor) from age 7 to 13 forgave him before he died, but she still struggles to forgive her mother, who allowed the abuse.

- A nurse asks, "How can we try to change a sick society that crusades to save whales and spotted owls, yet kills babies by the millions through abortion?"

Paul encourages us to put on the armor of God and take our place in the battle by using spiritual warfare. Prayer is an essential tactic if we want to walk in victory in our own lives and see that the gospel of Christ is made known in the earth.

God provides the Word of God—the Sword of the Spirit—as our primary weapon for confronting the enemy. Jesus wielded this very same weapon to push back the devil's assault in the wilderness temptation. He declared to Satan, "It is written . . ." and then quoted the Word to him three times (see Matthew 4:4-10; Luke 4:4-12). Today, Scripture remains our most powerful means of overcoming the evil one.

This book, a revised and improved version of the first edition, offers an arsenal of verses from both the Old and New Testaments to use in a variety of spiritual battles. Many believers deprive themselves of the help available in the Old Testament, thinking it is not applicable for today's world. But Paul wrote, "All Scripture is God-breathed and is useful for teaching, rebuking, correcting and training in righteousness, so that the man [or woman] of God may be thoroughly equipped for every good work" (2 Timothy 3:16-17).

The Word of God trains and equips us to be effective spiritual warriors. You also will find that by praying the Scriptures and declaring God's Word against enemy attacks, you can push back the powers of darkness and bring spiritual victory. At the same time, the Holy Spirit will work through the truth of Scripture to correct you, to nourish your spirit and to strengthen your faith.

This book is not a substitute for your Bible. But we trust that as you use this prayer guide, you will gain an even greater appreciation for the Word of God. May you increase your knowledge and skill in wielding this Sword of the Spirit, referred to by veteran missionary Arthur Mathews as *the soldier's best friend.*

Thanks be to God! He gives us the victory through our Lord Jesus Christ.
1 CORINTHIANS 15:57

—Quin Sherrer and Ruthanne Garlock

PROLOGUE

The apostle Paul wrote the most complete training guide for spiritual warriors:

> Be strong in the Lord and in his mighty power. Put on the full armor of God so that you can take your stand against the devil's schemes. For our struggle is not against flesh and blood, but against the rulers, against the authorities, against the powers of this dark world and against the spiritual forces of evil in the heavenly realms. Therefore put on the full armor of God, so that when the day of evil comes, you may be able to stand your ground, and after you have done everything, to stand. Stand firm then, with the belt of truth buckled around your waist, with the breastplate of righteousness in place, and with your feet fitted with the readiness that comes from the gospel of peace. In addition to all this, take up the shield of faith, with which you can extinguish all the flaming arrows of the evil one. Take the helmet of salvation and the sword of the Spirit, which is the word of God. And pray in the Spirit on all occasions with all kinds of prayers and requests. With this in mind, be alert and always keep on praying for all the saints (Ephesians 6:10-18).

Part I

PREPARING FOR BATTLE

PUTTING ON THE ARMOR

Even though Christ's decisive victory over Satan is complete, we need to acknowledge our own role in enforcing that victory through prayer and spiritual warfare. We face a very real enemy: Satan, whose name means "adversary." Since he knows that Christ is our only hope of deliverance from his kingdom of darkness, this foe is bent on preventing men, women and children from embracing the good news of salvation.

If we believers are to fulfill Christ's command to take the gospel to every creature, then we must give of our talents and treasure to further that cause. But we also must commit quality time to give ourselves to prayer and spiritual warfare on behalf of others.

Why the Armor Is Crucial

Only a fool would race into battle without adequate defense. A Christian likewise needs armor to provide protection against "the evil one"—a reference to Satan used in Scripture 24 times. Paul teaches believers to put on God's armor to stand our ground against the evil one (see Ephesians 6:13).

Jesus Himself taught His followers a model for prayer, which includes the petition "Deliver us from the evil one" (Matthew 6:13). In His own great priestly prayer for His followers, Jesus asked the Father to "protect them from the evil one" (John 17:15).

Spiritual warfare is far from being a struggle between two near-equal powers (God and Satan certainly are not equal in power). Rather, we define this warfare as Satan's efforts involving three basic elements:

1. To destroy believers' confidence in God and His Son, so they will forsake the faith.

2. To seduce believers through deceptive teaching or their own sin, so they will believe a lie instead of the truth.

3. To prevent unbelievers from hearing a clear presentation of the gospel, so they will remain in Satan's kingdom of darkness.

The devil has real power, which Christians would be wise to respect. E. M. Bounds affirms, "To Christ the devil was a very real person. He recognized his personality, felt and acknowledged his power, abhorred his character, and warred against his kingdom."[1] But because Satan is a created being in no way equal to God, his influence is limited. Through the cross, Christ disarmed Satan's power and secured victory for the believer who submits to Jesus' lordship (see Colossians 2:15).

How the Armor Functions

At the time Paul wrote about the armor of God, he was under house arrest, a prisoner of Rome guarded by Roman soldiers. Every day he saw the armor and insignia they wore, which identified their status. The Holy Spirit inspired the analogy of the believer as a soldier in God's spiritual army.

Just as a soldier must complete a period of training before being issued battle gear and sent to the front, so must we as Christian soldiers prepare ourselves for spiritual warfare before going to battle. Each piece of our spiritual armor serves a vital function; thus, missing a single part could mean defeat when encountering the enemy. May the Holy Spirit equip and strengthen us to be effective in our fight against Satan. Let's review the six pieces of the full armor presented by Paul in Ephesians 6:10-18.

The *belt of truth* was a wide leather or metal belt worn around the lower trunk to keep the armor in place, and to which the sword was attached. The truth of the gospel—salvation by faith in Christ alone—remains the crux of every battle we face. Satan distorts this truth in his attempt to make us doubt God and fall into deception. Jesus most vigorously warned against deception during the last days (see Matthew 24, Mark 13, Luke 21 and chapter 24 of this book).

The forerunner of the bulletproof vest, the *breastplate of righteousness*, protected the soldier's heart and other vital organs. This piece of armor is our only protection against a divided heart. A true soldier must heed Solomon's advice: "Above all else, guard your heart, for it is the wellspring of life" (Proverbs 4:23). If the devil can divide our hearts through footholds such as unforgiveness, selfishness and idolatry, then he gains a more secure position by which to defeat us.

The *shoes of peace* symbolize readiness. In oriental cultures, removing one's shoes was an act of reverence, mourning, or submission. When a soldier put on his shoes, it meant he was preparing to report for duty and face the enemy. As Christian soldiers, we wear our shoes of peace to invade enemy territory, bearing the good news and reconciling humankind to God. "He has committed to us the message of reconciliation" (2 Corinthians 5:19).

The *shield of faith* refers to the large rectangular shield a soldier used to deflect enemy blows coming from any direction. It was large enough to protect his entire body, as well as protect all the other pieces of armor. Often a soldier would anoint his shield with oil (analogous to an anointing of the Holy Spirit) in order to reflect the sun's rays and blind the enemy. Our steadfast faith in God will strengthen us in battle and enable us to resist the enemy and see him flee (see James 4:7; 1 Peter 5:8-9).

The *helmet of salvation* guards our minds against Satan's flaming arrows (see 1 Thessalonians 5:8). A soldier's helmet not only protected his head in battle but also bore the insignia of his army. Our renewed minds should so profoundly influence our behavior that those in the world will recognize we are Christians in both word and in deed. Keeping our minds renewed in Christ also protects us from deception.

The *sword of the Spirit* is used for both defense and offense. The better we know the Word of God, the more adept we will be at wielding this weapon to oppose the powers of evil. But as Arthur Mathews observes, "Unused weapons do not inflict casualties on the enemy nor win wars. . . . It is not enough to give mental assent to the fact that a spiritual warfare is going on. Passivity towards our enemy is what the devil wants from us and is his trick to cool the ardor of God's men of war."[2]

How Victory Is Assured

Scriptural warnings about "the evil one" and "the day of evil" should be taken seriously, but our assurance that everything we need to defeat the enemy has been provided through Christ should be taken just as seriously. It remains up to us to discipline ourselves, appropriate God's provision and march into battle. William Gurnall writes:

> To put on the armour of God . . . involves first and foremost a change of heart. The person who boasts that he has confidence in God but does not truly believe with his heart will never be safe in the war zone that separates earth and heaven. If by negligence or choice he fails to put on God's armour and rushes naked into battle, he signs his own death certificate. . . . Do not doubt for a moment that Satan will hurl all his fury at those who love God's Word. . . . If Satan was too crafty for man in his perfection, how much more dangerous [he is] to us now in our maimed condition—for we have never recovered from that first crack Adam's fall gave to our understanding.[3]

Wearing spiritual armor and praying the Word of God are not part of some sort of magic formula. Success is not guaranteed if certain words are spoken concerning a specific situation. Prayer and warfare must be solidly based upon faith in God and a relationship with the God whose Word we declare. "Dear friends, if our hearts do not condemn us, we have confidence before God and receive from him anything we ask, because we obey his commands and do what pleases him" (1 John 3:21-22).

The following verses will help spiritual warriors come to a place of faith and readiness so that their prayers can be truly powerful and effective.

Scriptures

May the words of my mouth and the meditation of my heart be pleasing in your sight, O LORD, my Rock and my Redeemer (Psalm 19:14).

"Not by might nor by power, but by my Spirit," says the LORD Almighty (Zechariah 4:6).

Watch and pray so that you will not fall into temptation. The spirit is willing, but the body is weak (Mark 14:38).

Then Jesus told his disciples a parable to show them that they should always pray and not give up (Luke 18:1).

"Why are you sleeping?" he asked them. "Get up and pray so that you will not fall into temptation" (Luke 22:46).

Therefore, I urge you, brothers, in view of God's mercy, to offer your bodies as living sacrifices, holy and pleasing to God—this is your spiritual act of worship (Romans 12:1).

The hour has come for you to wake up from your slumber, because our salvation is nearer now than when we first believed. The night is nearly over; the day is almost here. So let us put aside the deeds of darkness and put on the armor of light. . . . Clothe yourselves with the Lord Jesus Christ, and do not think about how to gratify the desires of the sinful nature (Romans 13:11-14).

For though we live in the world, we do not wage war as the world does. The weapons we fight with are not the weapons of the world. On the contrary, they have divine power to demolish strongholds (2 Corinthians 10:3-4).

Have nothing to do with the fruitless deeds of darkness, but rather expose them. . . . Be very careful, then, how you live—not as unwise but as wise, making the most of every opportunity, because the days are evil (Ephesians 5:11,15-16).

Devote yourselves to prayer, being watchful and thankful. And pray for us, too, that God may open a door for our message, so that we may proclaim the mystery of Christ, for which I [Paul] am in chains. Pray that I may proclaim it clearly, as I should (Colossians 4:2-4).

Fight the good fight of the faith. Take hold of the eternal life to which you were called when you made your good confession in the presence of many witnesses (1 Timothy 6:12).

Endure hardship with us like a good soldier of Christ Jesus. No one serving as a soldier gets involved in civilian affairs—he wants to please his commanding officer. . . . I [Paul] endure everything for the sake of the elect, that they too may obtain the salvation that is in Christ Jesus, with eternal glory (2 Timothy 2:3-4,10).

For the grace of God that brings salvation has appeared to all men. It teaches us to say "No" to ungodliness and worldly passions, and to live self-controlled, upright and godly lives in this present age (Titus 2:11-12).

Therefore, since we are surrounded by such a great cloud of witnesses, let us throw off everything that hinders and the sin that so easily entangles, and let us run with perseverance the race marked out for us. Let us fix our eyes on Jesus, the author and perfecter of our faith, who for the joy set before him endured the cross, scorning its shame, and sat down at the right hand of the throne of God (Hebrews 12:1-2).

Therefore, prepare your minds for action; be self-controlled; set your hope fully on the grace to be given you when Jesus Christ is revealed. As obedient children, do not conform to the evil desires you had when you lived in ignorance. But just as he who called you is holy, so be holy in all you do (1 Peter 1:13-15).

The end of all things is near. Therefore be clear minded and self-controlled so that you can pray (1 Peter 4:7).

Prayer

Lord, thank You for providing the spiritual armor I need to be an effective spiritual warrior. Because of my personal relationship with You, I am fully confident that You hear and will answer my prayers. Help me to daily be clothed with the full armor of God—the belt of truth, breastplate of righteousness, shoes of peace, shield of faith, helmet of salvation, and sword of the Spirit. May I be faithful in battle and determined never to give up, I pray in Jesus' name, amen.

TAKING AUTHORITY IN THE NAME OF JESUS

What did Jesus mean when He told His followers, "I have given you authority . . . to overcome all the power of the enemy" (Luke 10:19)? He was giving to believers the right to exercise power, in His name, over the power of Satan—God's enemy and ours.

One definition of authority is "the power to rule; the power of one whose will and commands must be obeyed by others."[1] In the beginning, God gave Adam the authority to rule, or to exercise power, in the Garden of Eden (see Genesis 2:15-20). Only one tree was declared off limits. But in yielding to Satan's temptation to eat the fruit of that tree, humankind went beyond the boundary of their God-given authority.

Now, sin would have power to rule over the human race. Why was the devil so determined to seduce men and women to sin? Bible teacher Dean Sherman clarifies:

> Satan wanted the authority God had given to man. Although he was on the planet, the devil did not have authority and jurisdiction over the planet. . . . Satan knew that man could use or misuse the authority given to him. When man disobeyed God, Satan was able to usurp man's authority. Just as God transferred some of his authority to man, so man passed it on to Satan . . . but Satan can only use it through man. He can only *influence* the world to the degree that man chooses to sin and live in disobedience to God. This is what we might call the balance of power.[2]

Relationship with Jesus

Through His sacrificial death, burial and resurrection, Christ defeated Satan's power and received from God authority over all angels and powers (see 1 Peter 3:18-22). Now humankind, through Christ, can regain the authority that Adam squandered. Dean Sherman explains further:

> The balance of power on the earth rests with man in the name of Jesus Christ. The authority is complete in man as long as man is in relationship with God through Jesus Christ. With our authority comes the responsibility to use it for God's purposes. If we don't rebuke the devil, he will not be rebuked. If we don't drive him back, he will not leave. It is up to us. Satan knows of our authority, but hopes we will stay ignorant. We must be as convinced of our authority as the devil is.[3]

Relationship is the key. Without a close relationship with Christ, we have no basis for taking authority over Satan and he knows it. But God has placed Christ at His own right hand in heaven in a position of authority over all other powers. And because we're a part of His body, the Church, we can use His name with authority. Scripture declares:

> His [God's] power is like the working of his mighty strength, which he exerted in Christ when he raised him from the dead and seated him at his right hand in the heavenly realms, far above all rule and authority, power and dominion, and every title that can be given, not only in the present age but also in the one to come. And God placed all things under his feet and appointed him to be head over everything for the church, which is his body (Ephesians 1:19-23).

The book of Acts records the story of a group of men who tried—to their sorrow—to cast out demons in the name of Jesus when they had no relationship with Him:

> Some Jews who went around driving out evil spirits tried to invoke the name of the Lord Jesus over those who were demon-

possessed. They would say, "In the name of Jesus, whom Paul preaches, I command you to come out." . . . One day the evil spirit answered them, "Jesus I know, and I know about Paul, but who are you?" Then the man who had the evil spirit jumped on them and overpowered them all. He gave them such a beating that they ran out of the house naked and bleeding (Acts 19:13-16).

Scriptures on Christ's God-Given Authority

In my vision at night I looked, and there before me was one like a son of man, coming with the clouds of heaven. He approached the Ancient of Days and was led into his presence. He was given authority, glory and sovereign power; all peoples, nations and men of every language worshiped him. His dominion is an everlasting dominion that will not pass away, and his kingdom is one that will never be destroyed (Daniel 7:13-14).

The crowds were amazed at his teaching, because he taught as one who had authority, and not as their teachers of the law (Matthew 7:28-29).

"So that you may know that the Son of Man has authority on earth to forgive sins. . . ." Then he said to the paralytic, "Get up, take your mat and go home." And the man got up and went home. When the crowd saw this, they were filled with awe; and they praised God, who had given such authority to men (Matthew 9:6-8).

The people were amazed at his teaching, because he taught them as one who had authority, not as the teachers of the law. . . . The people were all so amazed that they asked each other, "What is this? A new teaching—and with authority! He even gives orders to evil spirits and they obey him" (Mark 1:22,27).

"I lay down my life for the sheep. . . . No one takes it from me, but I lay it down of my own accord. I have authority to lay it down and authority to take it up again. This command I received from my Father" (John 10:15,18).

Therefore God exalted him [Christ] to the highest place and gave him the name that is above every name, that at the name of Jesus every knee should bow, in heaven and on earth and under the earth, and every tongue confess that Jesus Christ is Lord, to the glory of God the Father (Philippians 2:9-11).

He [Christ] is the image of the invisible God, the firstborn over all creation. For by him all things were created: things in heaven and on earth, visible and invisible, whether thrones or powers or rulers or authorities; all things were created by him and for him. He is before all things, and in him all things hold together. And he is the head of the body, the church; he is the beginning and the firstborn from among the dead, so that in everything he might have the supremacy (Colossians 1:15-18).

Praying for the Unprecedented

Few believers pray and exercise faith at the level Christ intended for His followers. J. Oswald Sanders challenges us to move up to the level of "audacious praying." He writes:

Seldom do our petitions rise above the level of natural thought or previous experience. Do we ever dare to pray for the unprecedented? The whole atmosphere of the age tends to make us minimize what we can expect of God, and yet His Word reveals that the extent of legitimate expectation is literally without limits. As though to anticipate our reluctance to ask audaciously, God employs every universal term in our language in his promises to the praying soul. Here they are: Whatsoever, wheresoever, whensoever, whosoever, all, any, every. . . . Trace [these] words in their relation to prayer and note how they encourage large petitions.[4]

Scriptures on Believers' Christ-Given Authority

The Lord will make you the head, not the tail. If you pay attention to the commands of the Lord your God that I give you this day and carefully follow them, you will always be at the top, never at the bottom (Deuteronomy 28:13).

I will give you the keys of the kingdom of heaven; whatever you bind on earth will be bound in heaven, and whatever you loose on earth will be loosed in heaven (Matthew 16:19).

Then Jesus came to them and said, "All authority in heaven and on earth has been given to me. Therefore go and make disciples of all nations, baptizing them in the name of the Father and of the Son and of the Holy Spirit, and teaching them to obey everything I have commanded you. And surely I am with you always, to the very end of the age" (Matthew 28:18-20).

When Jesus had called the Twelve together, he gave them power and authority to drive out all demons and to cure diseases, and he sent them out to preach the kingdom of God and to heal the sick (Luke 9:1-2).

I have given you authority to trample on snakes and scorpions and to overcome all the power of the enemy; nothing will harm you (Luke 10:19).

You did not choose me, but I chose you and appointed you to go and bear fruit—fruit that will last. Then the Father will give you whatever you ask in my name (John 15:16).

Jesus said, "Peace be with you! As the Father has sent me, I am sending you." And with that he breathed on them and said, "Receive the Holy Spirit" (John 20:21-22).

Through him and for his name's sake, we received grace and apostleship to call people from among all the Gentiles to the obedience that comes from faith. And you also are among those who are called to belong to Jesus Christ (Romans 1:5-6).

Unlike so many, we do not peddle the word of God for profit. On the contrary, in Christ we speak before God with sincerity, like men sent from God (2 Corinthians 2:17).

Whatever you do, whether in word or deed, do it all in the name of the Lord Jesus, giving thanks to God the Father through him (Colossians 3:17).

These, then, are the things you should teach. Encourage and rebuke with all authority. Do not let anyone despise you (Titus 2:15).

Submit yourselves, then, to God. Resist the devil, and he will flee from you (James 4:7).

To him who overcomes and does my will to the end, I will give authority over the nations . . . just as I have received authority from my Father (Revelation 2:26-27).

Prayer

Heavenly Father, thank You that Jesus paid the price to assure the enemy's certain defeat! Thank You that when we remain submitted to Christ, He invests us with the authority to use His name against the strategies of the evil one. Lord, strengthen me to do this with boldness and to see victories that will bring praise and honor to You alone. Thank You for the privilege of being Your representative in the earth. Amen.

THE POWER OF THE BLOOD OF JESUS

The blood of Jesus, the means of our redemption, is the most precious physical substance ever to touch the earth. In obedience to the law, the Jewish people had for generations offered animal sacrifices to atone for their sins and to satisfy the justice of God. But when Jesus came to earth, He fulfilled the law by becoming the perfect sacrifice, atoning for the sin of all humankind.

His blood is not only precious but also powerful, abolishing forever the need for animal sacrifice. Why did Jesus submit to a bloody death on a cross, when all the power of the universe was and is available to Him? The great expositor G. Campbell Morgan explains:

> He was not only the Sin-bearer; in the activities of that dark hour, he was the Sin-destroyer; in some infinite transaction beyond human power of thought, he destroyed the works of the devil. . . . In order to establish the Kingdom he must himself gather the sin to himself, and deal with it, grapple with it, master it, negate it; and, emerging from the struggle victorious, communicate life, in the power of which other souls shall be able to enter into the same struggle, and with a like result.[1]

When we confess our sins and repent of our rebellion against God, we receive forgiveness and cleansing through the blood of Jesus. His blood opens the door to reconciliation with the Father. It delivers us from the curse and power of sin, along with the fear of death, and assures Satan's ultimate defeat. It is also the basis of our authority over the enemy. H. A. Maxwell Whyte writes:

We can hardly claim to be under the Blood of Jesus if we are walking in deliberate disobedience. . . . Sprinkling of the Blood of Jesus without obedience to the Word of God will avail us nothing. . . . In the natural world, we would have no difficulty understanding how to apply disinfectant to an infection. We would take the disinfectant and sprinkle or pour it upon the infection, and the result would be that all germs and living organisms present in that infection would die. Now we should have no difficulty in doing the same thing spiritually. Wherever Satan is at work, we must apply the only corrective antidote there is—the Blood of Jesus. There is absolutely no alternative, no substitute. Prayer, praise, worship and devotion all have their part in our approach to God; but the Blood of Jesus is the only effective counteragent to corruption.[2]

To "apply the blood of Jesus" over ourselves and our loved ones in prayer and spiritual warfare is a way of declaring to the devil that Jesus' blood creates a boundary he cannot violate. Only believers who have by faith appropriated Christ's sacrifice for their sins can apply this precious blood. But we must not treat this as some magic formula that guarantees protection from adversity.

In fact, Jesus told His followers, "No servant is greater than his master. If they persecuted me, they will persecute you also" (John 15:20). And Paul wrote, "Everyone who wants to live a godly life in Christ Jesus will be persecuted" (2 Timothy 3:12).

Being under the blood of Jesus does mean that any attempt of the enemy to destroy us will ultimately end in Satan's own defeat, just as Jesus' death on the cross sealed Satan's doom. As we read in Scripture, "None of the rulers of this age understood it [God's wisdom], for if they had, they would not have crucified the Lord of glory" (1 Corinthians 2:8).

The practice of applying Jesus' blood is based upon the account in Exodus 12. God instructed the people of Israel to kill a sacrificial lamb and place the blood upon their doorframes, thereby protecting their households from the plague of death He would send upon the Egyptians. That lamb was a foreshadowing of the Lamb of God,

Jesus Himself, whose sacrifice at Calvary provided a way for all humankind to be delivered from spiritual death.

R. Arthur Mathews wrote, "Blessed is that intercessor who knows how to use the power of the blood in spiritual warfare."[3] You can do that by declaring aloud Scriptures that speak of the power of Jesus' blood.

Scriptures

The blood will be a sign for you on the houses where you are; and when I see the blood, I will pass over you. No destructive plague will touch you when I strike Egypt (Exodus 12:13).

For the life of a creature is in the blood, and I have given it to you to make atonement for yourselves on the altar; it is the blood that makes atonement for one's life (Leviticus 17:11).

Then he took the cup, gave thanks and offered it to them, saying, "Drink from it, all of you. This is my blood of the covenant, which is poured out for many for the forgiveness of sins" (Matthew 26:27-28).

Since we have now been justified by his blood, how much more shall we be saved from God's wrath through him! (Romans 5:9).

Therefore, whoever eats the bread or drinks the cup of the Lord in an unworthy manner will be guilty of sinning against the body and blood of the Lord. A man ought to examine himself before he eats of the bread and drinks of the cup (1 Corinthians 11:27-28).

In him we have redemption through his blood, the forgiveness of sins, in accordance with the riches of God's grace that he lavished on us with all wisdom and understanding (Ephesians 1:7-8).

Now in Christ Jesus you who once were far away have been brought near through the blood of Christ (Ephesians 2:13).

For God was pleased to have all his fullness dwell in him [Christ], and through him to reconcile to himself all things . . . by making peace through his blood, shed on the cross (Colossians 1:19-20).

Since the children have flesh and blood, he too shared in their humanity so that by his death he might destroy him who holds the power of death—that is, the devil (Hebrews 2:14).

He [Christ] did not enter by means of the blood of goats and calves; but he entered the Most Holy Place once for all by his own blood, having obtained eternal redemption. . . . How much more, then, will the blood of Christ, who through the eternal Spirit offered himself unblemished to God, cleanse our consciences from acts that lead to death, so that we may serve the living God! (Hebrews 9:12,14).

Without the shedding of blood there is no forgiveness. But now he [Christ] has appeared once for all at the end of the ages to do away with sin by the sacrifice of himself (Hebrews 9:22b,26b).

Since we have confidence to enter the Most Holy Place by the blood of Jesus, by a new and living way opened for us through the curtain, that is, his body . . . let us draw near to God with a sincere heart in full assurance of faith. . . . Let us hold unswervingly to the hope we profess, for he who promised is faithful (Hebrews 10:19-23).

For you know that it was not with perishable things such as silver or gold that you were redeemed . . . but with the precious blood of Christ, a lamb without blemish or defect. He was chosen before the creation of the world, but was revealed in these last times for your sake (1 Peter 1:18-20).

If we walk in the light, as he is in the light, we have fellowship with one another, and the blood of Jesus, his Son, purifies us from all sin (1 John 1:7).

The four living creatures and the twenty-four elders fell down before the Lamb. Each one had a harp and they were holding golden bowls full of incense, which are the prayers of the saints. And they sang a new song: "You are worthy to take the scroll and to open its seals, because you were slain, and with your blood you purchased men for God from every tribe and language and people and nation. You have made them to be a kingdom and priests to serve our God, and they will reign on the earth" (Revelation 5:8-10).

These are they who have come out of the great tribulation; they have washed their robes and made them white in the blood of the Lamb (Revelation 7:14).

They overcame him [Satan] by the blood of the Lamb and by the word of their testimony; they did not love their lives so much as to shrink from death (Revelation 12:11).

I saw heaven standing open and there before me was a white horse, whose rider is called Faithful and True. With justice he judges and makes war. His eyes are like blazing fire, and on his head are many crowns. He has a name written on him that no one knows but he himself. He is dressed in a robe dipped in blood, and his name is the Word of God (Revelation 19:11-13).

Prayer

Father God, thank You that Jesus was obedient to Your plan and willingly shed His blood to provide my redemption and defeat the enemy. I know that His blood is precious and powerful. As I apply the blood of Jesus over myself and my loved ones, I am declaring to the enemy that he cannot violate that boundary. I give You praise for the protection we have through the blood of Christ. Amen.

THE POWER OF THE WORD OF GOD

The only piece of the spiritual warrior's armor that is both offensive and defensive is named last on Paul's list: "the sword of the Spirit, which is the word of God" (Ephesians 6:17). William Gurnall aptly describes this piece of armor:

> The sword is the weapon continually used by soldiers to defend themselves and to rout their enemies. Thus it illustrates the most excellent use of God's Word, by which the believer both defends himself and cuts down his enemies. . . . Because Satan is a spirit we must fight him with spiritual arms. And the Word is a spiritual sword. . . . God's army overcomes every enemy by one of two ways—conversion or destruction. The Word of God is the sword which affects both—it has two edges.[1]

This two-edged sword is the very weapon Jesus used to withstand Satan in the wilderness. Jesus had studied Scripture from His boyhood and filled His mind with its truth. Thus, in the moment of crisis, His sword was sharp and ready. All it took to defeat the enemy was "every word that comes from the mouth of the LORD" (Deuteronomy 8:3).

Hebrews 4:12 particularly speaks of the power of the Word: "For the word of God is living and active. Sharper than any double-edged sword, it penetrates even to dividing soul and spirit, joints and marrow; it judges the thoughts and attitudes of the heart." Bible teacher Roy Hicks, Sr., offers this explanation of how we are to understand this:

> The term for "word" here [in Hebrews 4:12] is the Greek word *logos*, which commonly indicates the expression of a complete

idea and is used in referring to the Holy Scriptures. It contrasts with *rhema,* which generally refers to a word spoken or given. This recommends our understanding the difference between *all* the Bible and the *single* promise or promises the Holy Spirit may bring to our mind from the Word of God. When facing a situation of need, trial, or difficulty, the promises of God may become a *rhema* to you; that is, a weapon of the Spirit, "the word of God" [Ephesians 6:17]. Its authority is that this "word" comes from the Bible—God's Word—the completed *logos.*[2]

Scriptures

Then the LORD said to Moses, "Write down these words, for in accordance with these words I have made a covenant with you and with Israel" (Exodus 34:27).

If anyone does not listen to my words that the prophet speaks in my name, I myself will call him to account (Deuteronomy 18:19).

Take to heart all the words I have solemnly declared to you this day, so that you may command your children to obey carefully all the words of this law. They are not just idle words for you—they are your life (Deuteronomy 32:46-47).

When the king heard the words of the Book of the Law, he tore his robes. . . . "Go and inquire of the LORD for me and for the people and for all Judah about what is written in this book that has been found. Great is the LORD's anger that burns against us because our fathers have not obeyed the words of this book" (2 Kings 22:11-13).

They mocked God's messengers, despised his words and scoffed at his prophets until the wrath of the LORD was aroused against his people and there was no remedy (2 Chronicles 36:16).

My soul faints with longing for your salvation, but I have put my hope in your word. . . . Your word is a lamp to my feet and a light for my path. . . . Your statutes are my heritage forever; they are the joy of my heart. My heart is set on keeping your decrees to the very end (Psalm 119:81,105,111-12).

The unfolding of your words gives light; it gives understanding to the simple. . . . All your words are true; all your righteous laws are eternal (Psalm 119:130,160).

I will bow down toward your holy temple and will praise your name for your love and your faithfulness, for you have exalted above all things your name and your word (Psalm 138:2).

I [God] make known the end from the beginning, from ancient times, what is still to come. I say: My purpose will stand, and I will do all that I please. . . . What I have said, that will I bring about; what I have planned, that will I do (Isaiah 46:10-11).

So is my word that goes out from my mouth: It will not return to me empty, but will accomplish what I desire and achieve the purpose for which I sent it (Isaiah 55:11).

"Is not my word like fire," declares the LORD, "and like a hammer that breaks a rock in pieces?" (Jeremiah 23:29).

The LORD has done what he planned; he has fulfilled his word, which he decreed long ago. . . . Who can speak and have it happen if the Lord has not decreed it? (Lamentations 2:17; 3:37).

You must speak my words to them, whether they listen or fail to listen, for they are rebellious. . . . "None of my words will be delayed any longer; whatever I say will be fulfilled, declares the Sovereign LORD" (Ezekiel 2:7; 12:28).

By your words you will be acquitted, and by your words you will be condemned (Matthew 12:37).

Heaven and earth will pass away, but my words will never pass away (Matthew 24:35).

For with God nothing is ever impossible and no word from God shall be without power or impossible of fulfillment (Luke 1:37, *AMP*).

In the beginning was the Word, and the Word was with God, and the Word was God. . . . In him was life, and that life was the light of men (John 1:1,4).

I tell you the truth, whoever hears my word and believes him who sent me has eternal life and will not be condemned; he has crossed over from death to life. . . . If anyone keeps my word, he will never see death (John 5:24; 8:51).

"The Spirit gives life; the flesh counts for nothing. The words I have spoken to you are spirit and they are life. . . ." Simon Peter answered him, "Lord, to whom shall we go? You have the words of eternal life" (John 6:63,68).

Faith comes from hearing the message, and the message is heard through the word of Christ (Romans 10:17).

God's word is not chained (2 Timothy 2:9).

For you have been born again, not of perishable seed, but of imperishable, through the living and enduring word of God. For, ". . . the grass withers and the flowers fall, but the word of the Lord stands forever." And this is the word that was preached to you (1 Peter 1:23-25).

The word of God lives in you, and you have overcome the evil one (1 John 2:14).

These are the words of him who has the sharp, double-edged sword. . . . Repent therefore! Otherwise, I will soon come to you and will fight against them with the sword of my mouth (Revelation 2:12,16).

He who was seated on the throne said, "I am making everything new!" Then he said, "Write this down, for these words are trustworthy and true" (Revelation 21:5).

Prayer

Lord, I rejoice that the sword of the Spirit—the Word of God, our chief weapon—helps me to pray both defensively and offensively. Thank You, Jesus, for setting an example for us when You declared Scripture to defeat Satan in the wilderness. Teach me to wield this Sword of the Spirit with power in my prayers so that I may have victory over the enemy. In Your name, amen.

5

THE WEAPON
OF PRAISE

Praise, adulation, commendation—we heap such sentiments on people after they have achieved a goal or performed well in some way. But keen spiritual warriors learn the power of praising God *before* seeing evidence of His intervention in the matter they are praying about. We can offer thanksgiving with such confidence because of who He is—a God of love, faithfulness, holiness and justice.

Scripture declares, "He is the Rock, his works are perfect, and all his ways are just. A faithful God who does no wrong, upright and just is he" (Deuteronomy 32:4). When we praise God despite negative circumstances, we affirm His power and victory over those circumstances. Three important results flow from our praise:

1. God receives glory.
2. Our faith is increased and we are energized by the joy of the Lord that accompanies praise.
3. The enemy is terrified and his plans are confounded (see 2 Chronicles 20:22).

Since the devil knows the power of praise, he works diligently to discourage Christians from using this potent weapon against his dark kingdom. Jack R. Taylor writes:

Nothing terrifies the devil and his demons like praise. Praise brings the consciousness of the presence of God with all that accompanies it. The liars from the pit cannot effectively market their wares in an atmosphere of praise. Since it is a garment, we can make a choice to put it on as we do a shirt, a blouse, or a coat. The constant wearing of it will ward off the spirits of depression, discouragement, and despair. . . . Praise, the continuing exercise of heaven, is clearly etched into the memory of the devil and every other fallen angel. The memory of the aborted revolution, in which they all lost their lofty positions, is haunting and all too clear in their minds. . . . When they hear biblical praises they are driven to panic. They are irritated and devastated. . . . Their ranks are broken. Like metal scratching glass is the sound of praises to them.[1]

Paul and Silas, beaten and thrown into prison for casting a demon out of a slave girl, found praise most effective in the midst of a seemingly desperate situation (see Acts 16:16-36). They praised God in spite of the circumstances, knowing they could trust Him completely, no matter what the outcome. The enemy simply cannot overcome that kind of faith, and his plans are plunged into confusion.

Declare the following verses of praise from Scripture to set the enemy into confusion and to push back the forces of darkness and despair. Some of these passages can also be sung, which can multiply the effectiveness of praise.

Scriptures

I will sing to the LORD, for he is highly exalted. The horse and its rider he has hurled into the sea. The LORD is my strength and my song; he has become my salvation. He is my God, and I will praise him, my father's God, and I will exalt him (Exodus 15:1-2).

I call to the LORD, who is worthy of praise, and I am saved from my enemies. . . . I will praise you, O LORD, among the nations; I will sing praises to your name (2 Samuel 22:4,50).

Sing to him, sing praise to him; tell of all his wonderful acts. . . . For great is the LORD and most worthy of praise; he is to be feared above all gods. . . . Let the heavens rejoice, let the earth be glad; let them say among the nations, "The LORD reigns!" (1 Chronicles 16:9,25,31).

Praise be to you, O Lord, God of our father Israel, from everlasting to everlasting. Yours, O Lord, is the greatness and the power and the glory and the majesty and the splendor, for everything in heaven and earth is yours. Yours, O Lord, is the kingdom; you are exalted as head over all (1 Chronicles 29:10-11).

Jehoshaphat appointed men to sing to the Lord and to praise him for the splendor of his holiness as they went out at the head of the army, saying: "Give thanks to the Lord, for his love endures forever." As they began to sing and praise, the Lord set ambushes against the men . . . who were invading Judah, and they were defeated. . . . Then, led by Jehoshaphat, all the men of Judah and Jerusalem returned joyfully to Jerusalem, for the Lord had given them cause to rejoice over their enemies (2 Chronicles 20:21-22,27).

O Lord, our Lord, how majestic is your name in all the earth! You have set your glory above the heavens. From the lips of children and infants you have ordained praise because of your enemies, to silence the foe and the avenger (Psalm 8:1-2).

May the righteous be glad and rejoice before God; may they be happy and joyful. Sing to God, sing praise to his name, extol him who rides on the clouds—his name is the Lord—and rejoice before him (Psalm 68:3-4).

Sing to the Lord a new song; sing to the Lord, all the earth. Sing to the Lord, praise his name; proclaim his salvation day after day. Declare his glory among the nations, his marvelous deeds among all peoples. For great is the Lord and most worthy of praise; he is to be feared above all gods (Psalm 96:1-4).

Praise the Lord. Sing to the Lord a new song, his praise in the assembly of the saints. . . . Let them praise his name with dancing and make music to him with tambourine and harp. . . . May the praise of God be in their mouths and a double-edged sword in their hands, to inflict vengeance on the nations and punishment on the peoples, to bind their kings with fetters, their nobles with shackles of iron, to carry out the sentence written against them (Psalm 149:1-3,6-9).

Praise the LORD. Praise God in his sanctuary; praise him in his mighty heavens. Praise him for his acts of power; praise him for his surpassing greatness. Praise him with the sounding of the trumpet, praise him with the harp and lyre, praise him with tambourine and dancing, praise him with the strings and flute, praise him with the clash of cymbals, praise him with resounding cymbals. Let everything that has breath praise the LORD. Praise the LORD (Psalm 150).

O LORD, you are my God; I will exalt you and praise your name, for in perfect faithfulness you have done marvelous things. . . . In that day they will say, "Surely this is our God; we trusted in him, and he saved us. This is the LORD, we trusted in him; let us rejoice and be glad in his salvation" (Isaiah 25:1,9).

Sing to the LORD! Give praise to the LORD! He rescues the life of the needy from the hands of the wicked (Jeremiah 20:13).

Praise be to the name of God for ever and ever; wisdom and power are his. He changes times and seasons; he sets up kings and deposes them. He gives wisdom to the wise and knowledge to the discerning. He reveals deep and hidden things; he knows what lies in darkness, and light dwells with him. I thank and praise you, O God of my fathers (Daniel 2:20-23).

Though the fig tree does not bud and there are no grapes on the vines, though the olive crop fails and the fields produce no food, though there are no sheep in the pen and no cattle in the stalls, yet I will rejoice in the LORD, I will be joyful in God my Savior. The Sovereign LORD is my strength; he makes my feet like the feet of a deer, he enables me to go on the heights (Habakkuk 3:17-19).

And Mary said: "My soul glorifies the Lord and my spirit rejoices in God my Savior" (Luke 1:46-47).

At that time Jesus, full of joy through the Holy Spirit, said, "I praise you, Father, Lord of heaven and earth, because you have hidden these things from the wise and learned, and revealed them to little children" (Luke 10:21).

Praise be to the God and Father of our Lord Jesus Christ, who has blessed us in the heavenly realms with every spiritual blessing in Christ (Ephesians 1:3).

Through Jesus, therefore, let us continually offer to God a sacrifice of praise—the fruit of lips that confess his name (Hebrews 13:15).

To the only God our Savior be glory, majesty, power and authority, through Jesus Christ our Lord, before all ages, now and forevermore! Amen (Jude 25).

In a loud voice they sang: "Worthy is the Lamb, who was slain, to receive power and wealth and wisdom and strength and honor and glory and praise!" Then I heard every creature in heaven and on earth and under the earth and on the sea, and all that is in them, singing: "To him who sits on the throne and to the Lamb be praise and honor and glory and power, for ever and ever!" (Revelation 5:12-13).

Great and marvelous are your deeds, Lord God Almighty. Just and true are your ways, King of the ages. Who will not fear you, O Lord, and bring glory to your name? For you alone are holy. All nations will come and worship before you, for your righteous acts have been revealed (Revelation 15:3-4).

Prayer

Lord, strengthen me to praise You no matter what is going on around me. You have created all things. You have authority over all, and You alone are worthy to receive all praise and adoration. Teach me the power of praising You even before I see answers to my prayers. In my waiting times, help me to keep my eyes on You and not on circumstances. I know You are forever faithful! Amen.

6

AGREEMENT BRINGS BOLDNESS

"The wicked man flees though no one pursues, but the righteous are as bold as a lion" (Proverbs 28:1). *Bold as a lion.* That's what spiritual warriors are to be when standing against the enemy and calling upon the Lord for help.

Jesus tells a parable about a persistent man who goes at midnight to ask his neighbor for three loaves of bread for unexpected company. He knocks, knocks again and keeps on knocking. He states a specific request. Finally, the reluctant neighbor gets up and gives him the desired three loaves (see Luke 11:5-13).

Rather than being a story about how to attempt to overcome God's supposed reluctance to answer prayer, this parable concerns asking for a specific need with unashamed boldness and persistence. Jesus says, "Yet because of his shameless persistence and insistence he will get up and give him as much as he needs. So I say to you, Ask and keep on asking and it shall be given you; seek and keep on seeking and you shall find; knock and keep on knocking and the door shall be opened to you" (Luke 11:8-9, *AMP*). Bible teacher Jack Hayford says of this parable:

> The lesson revolves around one idea: shameless boldness. . . . Boldness is your privilege. Your assignment is to ask; his commitment is to give—as much as you need. Too many hesitate to pray. They hesitate through a sense of unworthiness, a feeling of distance from deity, a wondering about God's will in the matter . . . a fear that God won't hear. . . . Jesus strikes the death blow to such hesitancy: ask. Ask with unabashed forwardness; ask with shameless boldness, he commands. And when you

do, he clearly teaches, "Your friend, my Father, will rise to the occasion and see that everything you need is provided."[1]

The Power of Agreement

Your private prayer is important and potent, but praying with a prayer partner strengthens your effectiveness. Jesus encouraged us: "Again, I tell you that if two of you on earth agree about anything you ask for, it will be done for you by my Father in heaven. For where two or three come together in my name, there am I with them" (Matthew 18:19-20).

The word "agree" in this Scripture derives from a Greek word from which we get our English word "symphony." The Greek word means to be in harmony, or in accord, or to become one mind. Jesus was always in agreement with His heavenly Father, never doing or saying anything except what the Father instructed. In like manner, we can ask the Lord for His mind about a situation or problem and then pray in agreement with a prayer partner until we see results.

Remember that battles aren't always won instantly; we must be persistent. And each battle requires a different strategy—for that, we need the guidance and agreement of the Holy Spirit.

Ask the Lord for the right prayer support—be it one person or a team—who will agree in prayer with the way God has shown you to pray. Find partners who will remain steadfast and pray with you until victory is accomplished. Here are two illustrations of the power of agreement from Scripture:

About midnight Paul and Silas were praying and singing hymns to God, and the other prisoners were listening to them. Suddenly there was such a violent earthquake that the foundations of the prison were shaken. At once all the prison doors flew open, and everybody's chains came loose (Acts 16:25-26).

He [God] has delivered us [Paul, using editorial plural] from such a deadly peril, and he will deliver us. On him we have set our hope that he will continue to deliver us, as you help us by your prayers. Then many will give thanks on our behalf for

the gracious favor granted us in answer to the prayers of many
(2 Corinthians 1:10-11).

Angelic Intervention

Not only are we to pray boldly and in agreement, but we can also
count on God to send heavenly reinforcements: angels. We see several
accounts of His doing this in Scripture:

2 Kings 6:17	Elisha's servant sees invisible chariots protecting them.
Psalm 34:6-7	An angel comes to the aid of David.
Psalm 91:11	God promises to "command his angels" to protect His child.
Daniel 6:22	An angel shuts the mouths of the lions and delivers Daniel.
Daniel 10:5-14	An angel brings the answer to Daniel's prayer after encountering opposition from a satanic "prince."

Thomas B. White, in *The Believer's Guide to Spiritual Warfare*, explains:

The connection between prayer and angelic operation did not
cease in the early church. With Peter in prison (Acts 12), the
church prayed earnestly, and an angel came to set the Apostle
free. Acts 12:15 gives evidence of the possibility of guardian
angels. There is a connection between the calling and the out-
working of God's will. But we cannot know, nor should we
try to find out, the extent to which the angels are dependent
upon our prayers. . . . Our proper responsibility is to earnestly
pray and trust God to work. Our confidence must be that
when we pray in faith, the Lord hears and chooses the means
through which he will work.[2]

We can ask the Lord to intervene with angels—Scripture says they are "ministering spirits sent to serve those who will inherit salvation" (Hebrews 1:14). But we see no biblical support for the idea that we have the right to command angels to do our bidding. Sometimes in an emergency, however, we may cry out a prayer adapted from Psalm 91:11-12: "Lord, please dispatch Your angels to protect our son in that blinding snowstorm! Thank You for keeping him safe." The following are Scriptures you can pray in agreement with one or more prayer partners as the Holy Spirit directs your strategy for battle.

Scriptures

Moses answered the people, "Do not be afraid. Stand firm and you will see the deliverance the LORD will bring you to-day. The Egyptians you see today you will never see again" (Exodus 14:13).

Have I not commanded you? Be strong and courageous. Do not be terrified; do not be discouraged, for the LORD your God will be with you wherever you go (Joshua 1:9).

David said to the Philistine, "You come against me with sword and spear and javelin, but I come against you in the name of the LORD Almighty, the God of the armies of Israel, whom you have defied. This day the LORD will hand you over to me. . . . All those gathered here will know that it is not by sword or spear that the LORD saves; for the battle is the LORD'S, and he will give all of you into our hands" (1 Samuel 17:45-47).

It is God who arms me with strength and makes my way per-fect. He makes my feet like the feet of a deer; he enables me to stand on the heights. He trains my hands for battle; my arms can bend a bow of bronze. . . . You armed me with strength for battle; you made my adversaries bow at my feet. You made my enemies turn their backs in flight, and I destroyed my foes (2 Samuel 22:33-35,40-41).

"Don't be afraid," the prophet answered. "Those who are with us are more than those who are with them." And Elisha prayed, "O LORD, open his eyes so he may see." Then the LORD opened the servant's eyes, and he looked and saw the hills full of horses and chariots of fire all around Elisha (2 Kings 6:16-17).

You will not have to fight this battle. Take up your positions; stand firm and see the deliverance the LORD will give you, O Judah and Jerusalem. Do not be afraid; do not be discouraged. Go out to face them tomorrow, and the LORD will be with you (2 Chronicles 20:17).

The joy of the LORD is your strength (Nehemiah 8:10).

With your help I can advance against a troop; with my God I can scale a wall (Psalm 18:29).

When the storm has swept by, the wicked are gone, but the righteous stand firm forever (Proverbs 10:25).

Strengthen the feeble hands, steady the knees that give way; say to those with fearful hearts, "Be strong, do not fear; your God will come, he will come with vengeance; with divine retribution he will come to save you" (Isaiah 35:3-4).

I am the LORD, the God of all mankind. Is anything too hard for me? (Jeremiah 32:27).

But the people who know their God shall prove themselves strong and shall stand firm and do exploits [for God] (Daniel 11:32, *AMP*).

After this the Lord appointed seventy-two others and sent them two by two ahead of him to every town and place where he was about to go. He told them, "The harvest is plentiful, but the workers are few. Ask the Lord of the harvest, therefore, to send out workers into his harvest field. Go! I am sending you out like lambs among wolves" (Luke 10:1-3).

But you will receive power when the Holy Spirit comes on you; and you will be my witnesses in Jerusalem, and in all Judea and Samaria, and to the ends of the earth (Acts 1:8).

I appeal to you, brothers, in the name of our Lord Jesus Christ, that all of you agree with one another so that there may be no divisions among you and that you may be perfectly united in mind and thought (1 Corinthians 1:10).

Be on your guard; stand firm in the faith; be men of courage; be strong (1 Corinthians 16:13).

Let us not become weary in doing good, for at the proper time we will reap a harvest if we do not give up (Galatians 6:9).

Submit yourselves, then, to God. Resist the devil, and he will flee from you. . . . Be patient and stand firm, because the Lord's coming is near (James 4:7; 5:8).

Be self-controlled and alert. Your enemy the devil prowls around like a roaring lion looking for someone to devour. Resist him, standing firm in the faith, because you know that your brothers throughout the world are undergoing the same kind of sufferings (1 Peter 5:8-9).

Prayer

Lord, thank You that I can come fearlessly, boldly, confidently to You in prayer. Give me insight and understanding to pray what is on Your heart. Lord, help me always to pray according to Your will. Link me with prayer partners so that in agreement we can call forth Your plans and purposes. Thank You for the privilege of prayer! I give You praise, in Jesus' name, amen.

OTHER STRATEGIES FOR BATTLE

We now turn our attention to four other effective strategies in spiritual warfare: fasting, weeping, laughter and shouts of joy. Depending on what God wants to accomplish through us during a particular time of intercession, the Holy Spirit can guide us as to when to use each specific tool.

Fasting

Abstaining from food is a physical act but one having great spiritual significance. Coupled with prayer, it can be a powerful weapon in spiritual warfare. Once when the disciples could not cure a child suffering from seizures, Jesus told them that their ineffectiveness was due to their unbelief. Then he added, "This kind does not go out except by prayer and fasting" (Matthew 17:21, *NKJV*).

Jesus Himself fasted prior to momentous events in His ministry, and He clearly expected His followers to fast as well:

> When you fast, do not look somber as the hypocrites do. . . .
> But when you fast, put oil on your head and wash your face,
> so that it will not be obvious to men that you are fasting, but
> only to your Father, who is unseen; and your Father, who sees
> what is done in secret, will reward you (Matthew 6:16-18).

John's disciples chided Jesus because His disciples did not fast. Jesus replied that as long as the Bridegroom was with them, they need not fast. But when Jesus was taken away, then His followers would fast (see Matthew 9:14-15). That certainly includes us today. We see many other examples of fasting in the Bible:

David	2 Samuel 12:16; Psalm 109:24
Nehemiah	Nehemiah 1:4
Esther	Esther 4:16
Daniel	Daniel 9:3
God's people	Joel 1:14; 2:12
John's disciples	Matthew 9:14-15; Mark 2:18-22; Luke 5:33-39
Anna	Luke 2:37
Church at Antioch	Acts 13:2-3
Paul	2 Corinthians 11:27

Scripture declares the reason for fasting: "Is not this the kind of fasting I [God] have chosen: to loose the chains of injustice and untie the cords of the yoke, to set the oppressed free and break every yoke?" (Isaiah 58:6).

In addition to setting free the oppressed, fasting and prayer can also yield direction and answers from God, strategy for warfare, new revelation of Scripture, a closer walk with the Lord, a humbling of self, healing, and deliverance from evil spirits. In his book *God's Chosen Fast*, Arthur Wallis states:

> We must not think of fasting as a hunger strike designed to force God's hand and get our own way! Prayer, however, is more complex than simply asking a loving father to supply his child's needs. Prayer is warfare. Prayer is wrestling. There are opposing forces. There are spiritual cross currents.... The man who prays with fasting is giving heaven notice that he is truly in earnest; that he will not give up nor let God go without the blessing.[1]

Individual Fasts

When you fast, be sure to pray and read Scripture. Allow time for God to speak to you, either through the Word or by the still, small voice of

Once, when the people of Judah were suffering under God's judgment for disobedience, God told Joel to call the people to fasting and repentance:

> Declare a holy fast; call a sacred assembly. Summon the elders and all who live in the land to the house of the LORD your God, and cry out to the LORD (Joel 1:14).

> "Even now," declares the LORD, "return to me with all your heart, with fasting and weeping and mourning." Rend your heart and not your garments. Return to the LORD your God, for he is gracious and compassionate, slow to anger and abounding in love, and he relents from sending calamity. Who knows? He may turn and have pity and leave behind a blessing—grain offerings and drink offerings for the LORD your God. Blow the trumpet in Zion, declare a holy fast, call a sacred assembly (Joel 2:12-15).

Prayer for Fasting

Lord, help me heed Your call to fast and pray and seek
Your direction. I know fasting can accomplish much in me,
as well as in the situation or people for whom I'm interceding.
Grant guidance for how long to fast and for Your strength to do it.
My spirit is willing, but my body is often frail. Give me
Your wisdom, Lord, and help me to glorify You through
my fasting. In Jesus' name, amen.

Weeping

God promises, "Those who sow in tears will reap with songs of joy. He who goes out weeping, carrying seed to sow, will return with songs of joy, carrying sheaves with him" (Psalm 126:5-6.) Dick Eastman, popular teacher on prayer and intercession, comments on this psalm:

> Tears in Scripture play a unique role in spiritual breakthrough. Here we discover that the planting of seeds accompanied by a spirit of brokenness will not only bring a spiritual harvest

the Holy Spirit whispering in your heart. The prophet Dai
his experience with fasting:

> So I turned to the Lord God and pleaded with him in
> and petition, in fasting, and in sackcloth and ashes. W
> was speaking and praying, confessing my sin and the si
> my people Israel and making my request to the LORD
> Gabriel, the man I had seen in the earlier vision, came to
> in swift flight about the time of the evening sacrifice. He i
> structed me and said to me, "Daniel, I have now come to giv
> you insight and understanding" (Daniel 9:3,20-22).

If for health reasons you cannot go on an extended fast, you c
try a modified fast, or you can give up a favorite food or activity as a
act of denying yourself during a specific period set aside for praye
Start with one-day to three-day fasts before attempting a prolonged
period, and drink lots of water or diluted clear juices while fasting.
The motive of the heart is more important than the length of the fast.
The important thing is openness and obedience to the voice of the
Holy Spirit.

Expect opposition from Satan when you enter a fast. He attacked
Jesus in the wilderness and tempted Him to turn stones into bread after His forty days without food. Ask God for strength to overcome attacks of weakness, exaggerated hunger pangs, nausea or headaches.
Just as Jesus answered the tempter by quoting the Word of God, we
can do the same: "Man does not live on bread alone, but on every word
that comes from the mouth of God" (Matthew 4:4).

Collective Fasts

When a coalition of enemies determined to attack the people of Judah, messengers brought word of it to King Jehoshaphat. Alarmed
by this news, Scripture says the king "resolved to inquire of the LORD,
and he proclaimed a fast for all Judah" (2 Chronicles 20:3). God responded to their fasting, confession and prayer of agreement by giving them a strategy to prevail over their enemies. (See the entire chapter
in 2 Chronicles for the inspiring story of this victory.)

of results, but will leave the sower with a spirit of rejoicing in the process. This passage, along with numerous others in Scripture regarding a spirit of brokenness, pictures a variety of purposes and functions related to what might be termed "the ministry of tears," a ministry Charles H. Spurgeon defined as "liquid prayer."[2]

Eastman goes on to mention six different types of tears:

1. Tears of sorrow or suffering (2 Kings 20:5)
2. Tears of joy (Genesis 33:4)
3. Tears of compassion (John 11:35)
4. Tears of desperation (Esther 4:1,3)
5. Tears of travail (Isaiah 42:14)
6. Tears of repentance (Joel 2:12-13)[3]

In our quiet times with the Lord, we may find ourselves weeping or in travail as we pray. Our weeping could be due to any of the above reasons. This modern translation of one of David's psalms of lament shows that our tears are valuable to God:

> You keep track of all my sorrows. You have collected all my tears in your bottle. You have recorded each one in your book. My enemies will retreat when I call to you for help. This I know: God is on my side (Psalm 56:8-9, *NLT*).

Scriptures on Weeping

Streams of tears flow from my eyes, for your law is not obeyed (Psalm 119:136).

The Sovereign Lord will wipe away the tears from all faces; he will remove the disgrace of his people from all the earth. The Lord has spoken (Isaiah 25:8).

Oh, that my head were a spring of water and my eyes a fountain of tears! I would weep day and night for the slain of my people (Jeremiah 9:1).

But if you do not listen, I will weep in secret because of your pride; my eyes will weep bitterly, overflowing with tears, because the LORD's flock will be taken captive (Jeremiah 13:17).

This is what the LORD says: "Restrain your voice from weeping and your eyes from tears, for your work will be rewarded," declares the LORD. "They will return from the land of the enemy" (Jeremiah 31:16).

Let the priests, who minister before the LORD, weep between the temple porch and the altar. Let them say, "Spare your people, O LORD. Do not make your inheritance an object of scorn, a byword among the nations. Why should they say among the peoples, 'Where is their God?'" (Joel 2:17).

Blessed are those who mourn, for they will be comforted (Matthew 5:4).

Rejoice with those who rejoice; mourn with those who mourn (Romans 12:15).

For I wrote you out of great distress and anguish of heart and with many tears, not to grieve you but to let you know the depth of my love for you (2 Corinthians 2:4).

During the days of Jesus' life on earth, he offered up prayers and petitions with loud cries and tears to the one who could save him from death, and he was heard because of his reverent submission (Hebrews 5:7).

Come near to God and he will come near to you. Wash your hands, you sinners, and purify your hearts, you double-minded. Grieve, mourn and wail. Change your laughter to mourning and your joy to gloom. Humble yourselves before the Lord, and he will lift you up (James 4:8-10).

Prayer for Weeping

Lord, You see my tears as I identify with the hurting, lost ones for whom I intercede. Give me a heart of compassion, and help me to pray with discernment and wisdom for the ones You put on my heart. Receive my tears as intercession for their deepest needs, Lord, and reveal to them Your love and truth. In Jesus' name, amen.

Scornful Laughter

Laughter may seem a strange warfare strategy. But when we can laugh in spite of the enemy's activity against us, we'll quickly put him to flight. Often in the Bible, laughter is used to express mockery, derision or scorn—a very appropriate stance toward Satan. When a powerful enemy king threatened to conquer all the land of Judah, King Hezekiah prayed for deliverance and asked God to vindicate His name. The Lord responded through the prophet Isaiah with this word:

> This is the word which the LORD has spoken concerning him [the king of Assyria]: "The virgin, the daughter of Zion, has despised you, laughed you to scorn. The daughter of Jerusalem has shaken her head behind your back! Whom have you reproached and blasphemed? Against whom have you raised your voice and lifted up your eyes on high? Against the Holy One of Israel" (2 Kings 19:21-22, *NKJV*).

The Holy Spirit may direct spiritual warriors to laugh in scorn at the devil's plan. An African proverb says, "When a mouse laughs at a cat, there must be a hole nearby." The enemy may seem bigger and stronger than we are, but we can rely on God's almighty power to deliver us.

A pastor notes, "God named Abraham's son Isaac, which means laughter, and the Bible often refers to Jehovah as the God of Isaac (laughter). When Abraham first heard the promise that he'd have a son though he was 100 years old, he fell down laughing [see Genesis 17:17]. Not just a chuckle. It was Holy Spirit 'belly laughter.'"

Sarah also "laughed to herself as she thought, 'After I am worn out and my master is old, will I now have this pleasure?'" (Genesis 18:12). Later, after Isaac was born, she said, "God has brought me laughter, and everyone who hears about this will laugh with me" (Genesis 21:6).

Scriptures on Scornful Laughter

The One enthroned in heaven laughs; the LORD scoffs at them (Psalm 2:4).

The wicked plot against the righteous and gnash their teeth at them; but the Lord laughs at the wicked, for he knows their day is coming (Psalm 37:12-13).

The righteous will see and fear; they will laugh at him, saying, "Here now is the man who did not make God his stronghold but trusted in his great wealth and grew strong by destroying others!" But I am like an olive tree flourishing in the house of God; I trust in God's unfailing love for ever and ever (Psalm 52:6-8).

See what they [wicked nations] spew from their mouths—they spew out swords from their lips, and they say, "Who can hear us?" But you, O LORD, laugh at them; you scoff at all those nations (Psalm 59:7-8).

Joyful Laughter

Other scriptural references to laughter appear to mark occasions of gratification and/or restored joy. Paul wrote, "Rejoice in the Lord always. I will say it again: Rejoice!" (Philippians 4:4). Sarah was gratified and rejoiced to finally have a child, and there are other examples of women in the Bible who rejoiced, including Miriam (see Exodus 15:20-21), Hannah see (1 Samuel 2:1-10) and Mary (see Luke 1:46-55).

Scriptures on Joyful Laughter

He will yet fill your mouth with laughter and your lips with shouts of joy. Your enemies will be clothed in shame, and the tents of the wicked will be no more (Job 8:21-22).

A cheerful heart is good medicine, but a crushed spirit dries up the bones (Proverbs 17:22).

There is a time for everything, and a season for every activity under heaven: . . . a time to weep and a time to laugh, a time to mourn and a time to dance (Ecclesiastes 3:1-4).

Blessed are you who hunger now, for you will be satisfied. Blessed are you who weep now, for you will laugh (Luke 6:21).

Shouts of Joy

A shout can be anything from an acclamation of joy to a battle cry—a decisive declaration of victory. It can be a crashing sound, a loud clamor or a cry of excitement.

Joshua ordered the Israelites to march around the walls of Jericho in silence for six days. But on the seventh day, after marching around seven times, the walls collapsed when they shouted at his command: "Shout! For the LORD has given you the city!" (Joshua 6:16). What a glorious shout that must have been!

Scripture declares this about Jesus' return: "For the Lord Himself will descend from heaven with a shout, with the voice of an archangel, and with the trumpet of God" (1 Thessalonians 4:16, *NKJV*). How glorious and joyful that declaration of victory will be!

Scriptures on Shouts of Joy

And on that day they offered great sacrifices, rejoicing because God had given them great joy. The women and children also rejoiced. The sound of rejoicing in Jerusalem could be heard far away (Nehemiah 12:43).

Then my head will be exalted above the enemies who surround me; at his tabernacle will I sacrifice with shouts of joy; I will sing and make music to the LORD (Psalm 27:6).

Clap your hands, all you nations; shout to God with cries of joy. How awesome is the LORD Most High, the great King over all the earth! . . . God has ascended amid shouts of joy, the LORD amid the sounding of trumpets (Psalm 47:1-2,5).

Come, let us sing for joy to the LORD; let us shout aloud to the Rock of our salvation (Psalm 95:1).

He brought out his people with rejoicing, his chosen ones with shouts of joy (Psalm 105:43).

Shouts of joy and victory resound in the tents of the righteous: "The LORD's right hand has done mighty things!" (Psalm 118:15).

Our mouths were filled with laughter, our tongues with songs of joy. Then it was said among the nations, "The LORD has done great things for them" (Psalm 126:2).

Prayer for Laughter and Shouts of Joy

Lord, thank You for the gift of laughter! Show us when to laugh in scorn at the enemy in our warfare, as You bring deliverance and victory through Your mighty hand. Thank You for the times when we can shout for joy and take spoils from the enemy. We praise You for Your mighty works! In Jesus' name, amen.

ASSURED OF VICTORY

Spiritual warriors need to remind themselves and the enemy that his defeat is an irreversible fact. This is best done by wielding the proclamations of God's Word against our adversary, whose ruin was sealed at the cross. Arthur Mathews affirms this:

> Satan is a defeated foe, with a crushed head. There is no power in him, nor are there any means available to him to reach and unseat the Victor of Calvary now seated at the right hand of the Father. It is not for us to fight *for* victory. . . . Our fight is *from* victory; and from this vantage point, empowered with Christ's might, and completely enclosed in the whole armor of God, the powers of evil are compelled to back off as we resist them.[1]

Scripture encourages us to look beyond the difficult or seemingly impossible state of affairs that Satan uses to try to weaken our faith. We must fix our spiritual eyes on Jesus—"the author and perfecter of our faith" (Hebrews 12:2)—who secures the victory. By believing the promises of God instead of the lies of the enemy, we cooperate with God's plan for triumph and confound the enemy's plan. Our faith, anchored in God's Word, need not be shaken by circumstances. Puritan author William Gurnall wrote:

> I am not to believe what the Word says merely because it agrees with my reason; but I must believe my reason because it aligns with the Word. A carpenter lays his rule to the plank and sees it to be straight or crooked; yet it is not the eye but the rule that is the measure. He can always trust his rule to be right.[2]

Our assurance of victory over Satan is based upon the integrity and infallibility of God's Word, not upon our interpretation of circumstances. Use the following verses of Scripture to verbally declare your faith in God's promise and in His power to fulfill that promise. Your declaration of victory will immobilize the enemy's attack.

Scriptures Declaring God's Promises

The LORD was gracious to Sarah as he had said, and the LORD did for Sarah what he had promised (Genesis 21:1).

For the LORD your God is the one who goes with you to fight for you against your enemies to give you victory. . . . The LORD will grant that the enemies who rise up against you will be defeated before you. They will come at you from one direction but flee from you in seven (Deuteronomy 20:4; 28:7).

The eternal God is your refuge, and underneath are the everlasting arms. He will drive out your enemy before you, saying, "Destroy him!" (Deuteronomy 33:27).

The LORD will march out like a mighty man, like a warrior he will stir up his zeal; with a shout he will raise the battle cry and will triumph over his enemies (Isaiah 42:13).

Before they call I will answer; while they are still speaking I will hear (Isaiah 65:24).

For nothing is impossible with God. . . . Blessed is she who has believed that what the Lord has said to her will be accomplished! (Luke 1:37,45).

If you remain in me and my words remain in you, ask whatever you wish, and it will be given you. This is to my Father's glory, that you bear much fruit, showing yourselves to be my disciples (John 15:7-8).

For he [Christ] must reign until he has put all his enemies under his feet. The last enemy to be destroyed is death.... then the saying that is written will come true: "Death has been swallowed up in victory." "Where, O death, is your victory? Where, O death, is your sting?" The sting of death is sin, and the power of sin is the law. But thanks be to God! He gives us the victory through our Lord Jesus Christ (1 Corinthians 15:25-26,54-56).

Scriptures Declaring God's Power

Your right hand, O LORD, was majestic in power. Your right hand, O LORD, shattered the enemy.... The enemy boasted, "I will pursue, I will overtake them. I will divide the spoils; I will gorge myself on them. I will draw my sword and my hand will destroy them." But you blew with your breath, and the sea covered them. They sank like lead in the mighty waters (Exodus 15:6,9-10).

I am the LORD, who has made all things, ... who foils the signs of false prophets and makes fools of diviners, who overthrows the learning of the wise and turns it into nonsense, who carries out the words of his servants and fulfills the predictions of his messengers (Isaiah 44:24-26).

He [Abraham] faced the fact that his body was as good as dead ... and that Sarah's womb was also dead. Yet he did not waver through unbelief regarding the promise of God, but was strengthened in his faith and gave glory to God, being fully persuaded that God had power to do what he had promised (Romans 4:19-21).

I pray also that the eyes of your heart may be enlightened in order that you may know ... his incomparably great power for us who believe. That power is like the working of his mighty strength, which he exerted in Christ when he raised him from the dead and seated him at his right hand in the heavenly realms, far above all rule and authority, power and dominion, and every title that can be given, not only in the present age but also in the one to come. And God placed all things under his feet and appointed him to be head over everything for the church (Ephesians 1:18-22).

Scriptures Declaring God's Justice

Will not the Judge of all the earth do right? (Genesis 18:25).

Those who oppose the LORD will be shattered. He will thunder against them from heaven; the LORD will judge the ends of the earth (1 Samuel 2:10).

Now let the fear of the LORD be upon you. Judge carefully, for with the LORD our God there is no injustice or partiality or bribery (2 Chronicles 19:7).

He will judge the world in righteousness; he will govern the peoples with justice (Psalm 9:8).

Your throne, O God, will last for ever and ever; a scepter of justice will be the scepter of your kingdom (Psalm 45:6).

Say among the nations, "The LORD reigns." The world is firmly established, it cannot be moved; he will judge the peoples with equity (Psalm 96:10).

For God will bring every deed into judgment, including every hidden thing, whether it is good or evil (Ecclesiastes 12:14).

And he [Messiah] will delight in the fear of the LORD. He will not judge by what he sees with his eyes, or decide by what he hears with his ears; but with righteousness he will judge the needy, with justice he will give decisions for the poor of the earth (Isaiah 11:3-4).

Yet the LORD longs to be gracious to you; he rises to show you compassion. For the LORD is a God of justice. Blessed are all who wait for him! (Isaiah 30:18).

God presented him [Jesus] as a sacrifice of atonement, through faith in his blood. He did this to demonstrate his justice (Romans 3:25).

See, the Lord is coming with thousands upon thousands of his holy ones to judge everyone, and to convict all the ungodly of all the ungodly acts they have done in the ungodly way, and of all the harsh words ungodly sinners have spoken against him (Jude 14-15).

Scriptures Declaring Victory

It was not by their sword that they won the land, nor did their arm bring them victory; it was your right hand, your arm, and the light of your face, for you loved them. . . . I do not trust in my bow, my sword does not bring me victory; but you give us victory over our enemies, you put our adversaries to shame. In God we make our boast all day long, and we will praise your name forever (Psalm 44:3,6-8).

With God we will gain the victory, and he will trample down our enemies (Psalm 60:12).

Your arm is endued with power; your hand is strong, your right hand exalted. Righteousness and justice are the foundation of your throne; love and faithfulness go before you (Psalm 89:13-14).

Do not gloat over me, my enemy! Though I have fallen, I will rise. Though I sit in darkness, the LORD will be my light. . . . Then my enemy will see it and will be covered with shame (Micah 7:8-10).

Everyone born of God overcomes the world. This is the victory that has overcome the world, even our faith. . . . This is the confidence we have in approaching God: that if we ask anything according to his will, he hears us. And if we know that he hears us—whatever we ask—we know that we have what we asked of him (1 John 5:4,14-15).

Prayer

Thank You, Lord, that as we pray and do battle according to Your will, we know triumph is assured. Give me strength to stand in faith, knowing Your power is greater than all the power of the evil one. I lift up a shout of praise to declare that the victory is won in Jesus' name, amen.

PART II

WINNING YOUR PERSONAL BATTLES

9

ASSURANCE OF SALVATION

Satan, our enemy, constantly accuses us before God (see Revelation 12:10) and seeks to destroy our confidence in Christ by causing us to doubt our salvation.

Many Christians suffer great mental anguish over the question, How can I know whether I'm truly born again? Their sense of unworthiness and guilt often drive them to try to earn salvation through good works or penance. Or they completely give up on trying to be a Christian, feeling they can never meet the qualifications.

This reaction actually cooperates with Satan's desire to nullify the power of Christ's sacrificial death, burial and resurrection. If it were possible to *earn* salvation, we wouldn't need a savior!

God's Word clearly teaches that we are reborn by confessing our sins, declaring our faith in Christ, and receiving forgiveness and cleansing through His grace. The transaction occurs instantly. However, growing into maturity and exhibiting the fruits of the Spirit require time and patience in learning Scripture and applying it to our lives.

T. W. Wilson explains the meaning of "atonement":

> The Old Testament Hebrew word that we translate "atonement" means literally "to cover up." The animal sacrifices were intended to "cover" a man's sins. In the New Testament, however, the meaning of atoning sacrifice is conveyed by the word "expiate," which means "to put away." The blood that Jesus shed in our behalf on the cross at Calvary does not merely cover up our sin; it puts away our sin as though it had never been committed.[1]

When you stumble and fall in your walk with the Lord, as Peter did, you can always repent and get on your feet again. Don't believe the lie that God has rejected you! Peter was forgiven and went on to become a major leader of the Early Church. When the enemy bombards your mind with doubt, use the following verses to proclaim your salvation.

Scriptures

The LORD is my light and my salvation—whom shall I fear? The LORD is the stronghold of my life—of whom shall I be afraid? (Psalm 27:1).

We have sinned, even as our fathers did; we have done wrong and acted wickedly. . . . Yet he saved them for his name's sake, to make his mighty power known. . . . He saved them from the hand of the foe; from the hand of the enemy he redeemed them (Psalm 106:6-10).

In that day they will say, "Surely this is our God; we trusted in him, and he saved us. This is the LORD, we trusted in him; let us rejoice and be glad in his salvation" (Isaiah 25:9).

We all, like sheep, have gone astray, each of us has turned to his own way; and the LORD has laid on him the iniquity of us all. After the suffering of his soul, he will see the light [of life] and be satisfied; by his knowledge my righteous servant will justify many, and he will bear their iniquities (Isaiah 53:6,11).

All men will hate you because of me, but he who stands firm to the end will be saved. . . . Whoever believes and is baptized will be saved, but whoever does not believe will be condemned (Mark 13:13; 16:16).

Do not rejoice that the spirits submit to you, but rejoice that your names are written in heaven. . . . For the Son of Man came to seek and to save what was lost (Luke 10:20; 19:10).

For God so loved the world that he gave his one and only Son, that whoever believes in him shall not perish but have eternal life. For God did not send his Son into the world to condemn the world, but to save the world through him (John 3:16-17).

I tell you the truth, whoever hears my word and believes him who sent me has eternal life and will not be condemned; he has crossed over from death to life (John 5:24).

Then you will know the truth, and the truth will set you free. . . . So if the Son sets you free, you will be free indeed (John 8:32,36).

I am the gate; whoever enters through me will be saved. . . . I give them eternal life, and they shall never perish; no one can snatch them out of my hand (John 10:9,28).

Everyone who calls on the name of the Lord will be saved. . . . Salvation is found in no one else, for there is no other name under heaven given to men by which we must be saved (Acts 2:21; 4:12).

I am not ashamed of the gospel, because it is the power of God for the salvation of everyone who believes (Romans 1:16).

But now a righteousness from God, apart from law, has been made known. . . . This righteousness from God comes through faith in Jesus Christ to all who believe. There is no difference, for all have sinned and fall short of the glory of God, and are justified freely by his grace through the redemption that came by Christ Jesus (Romans 3:21-24).

But now that you have been set free from sin and have become slaves to God, the benefit you reap leads to holiness, and the result is eternal life. For the wages of sin is death, but the gift of God is eternal life in Christ Jesus our Lord (Romans 6:22-23).

Therefore, there is now no condemnation for those who are in Christ Jesus, because through Christ Jesus the law of the Spirit of life set me free from the law of sin and death (Romans 8:1-2).

If you confess with your mouth, "Jesus is Lord," and believe in your heart that God raised him from the dead, you will be saved. For it is with your heart that you believe and are justified, and it is with your mouth that you confess and are saved (Romans 10:9-10).

Therefore, if anyone is in Christ, he is a new creation; the old has gone, the new has come! (2 Corinthians 5:17).

I have been crucified with Christ and I no longer live, but Christ lives in me. The life I live in the body, I live by faith in the Son of God, who loved me and gave himself for me (Galatians 2:20).

But because of his great love for us, God, who is rich in mercy, made us alive with Christ even when we were dead in transgressions. . . . For it is by grace you have been saved, through faith—and this not from yourselves, it is the gift of God—not by works, so that no one can boast (Ephesians 2:4-5,8-9).

But when the kindness and love of God our Savior appeared, he saved us, not because of righteous things we had done, but because of his mercy. He saved us through the washing of rebirth and renewal by the Holy Spirit (Titus 3:4-5).

In bringing many sons to glory, it was fitting that God, for whom and through whom everything exists, should make the author of their salvation perfect through suffering. . . . And, once made perfect, he became the source of eternal salvation for all who obey him (Hebrews 2:10; 5:9).

Because Jesus lives forever, he has a permanent priesthood. Therefore he is able to save completely those who come to God through him, because he always lives to intercede for them. Such a high priest meets our need—one who is holy, blameless, pure, set apart from sinners, exalted above the heavens. Unlike the other high priests, he does not need to offer sacrifices day after day, first for his own sins, and then for the sins of the people. He sacrificed for their sins once for all when he offered himself (Hebrews 7:24-27).

Since we have a great priest over the house of God, let us draw near to God with a sincere heart in full assurance of faith, having our hearts sprinkled to cleanse us from a guilty conscience and having our bodies washed with pure water. Let us hold unswervingly to the hope we profess, for he who promised is faithful (Hebrews 10:21-23).

If we confess our sins, he is faithful and just and will forgive us our sins and purify us from all unrighteousness (1 John 1:9).

After this I heard what sounded like the roar of a great multitude in heaven shouting: "Hallelujah! Salvation and glory and power belong to our God. . . ." Then I heard what sounded like a great multitude, like the roar of rushing waters and like loud peals of thunder, shouting: "Hallelujah! For our Lord God Almighty reigns. Let us rejoice and be glad and give him glory! For the wedding of the Lamb has come, and his bride has made herself ready. Fine linen, bright and clean, was given her to wear" (Revelation 19:1,6-8).

Prayer

Father, thank You that when Jesus shed His blood on the cross He provided a way for my sins to be removed. I ask Your forgiveness for the times when I have failed to obey Your Word. I accept Jesus' sacrifice for me; I receive Your forgiveness and cleansing, and reaffirm my faith in You. Father, I praise You for the free gift of salvation—I don't have to earn it! Help me to walk in Your ways and daily acknowledge the Lordship of Jesus in my life.
In His name, amen.

10

OVERCOMING DEPRESSION AND BURNOUT

Depression and burnout are to the mind what sickness and disease are to the body. This emotional malady is a growing problem in the wake of modern society's relentless pursuit of success and achievement. Psychologist and author Dr. Archibald Hart observes:

> A culture such as ours, where there is a high priority placed on performance and success as symbols of worthiness and where there is a diminishing opportunity to be successful, is bound to give rise to an increased gap between expectations and accomplishments. This in turn creates disillusionment. . . . Equally important is the increasing abuse and misuse of the body. *Stress* is the key word explaining this abuse. The more complex a culture, the greater is the experience of stress. The consequent physiological distress plays havoc with the biochemical processes of the body, and depression is a symptom and the natural outcome of this distress.[1]

Some cases of depression may be caused by an imbalance in the body's chemistry, side effects of medication, or insufficient nutrition. Usually a combination of physical, emotional and spiritual factors come into play. Sinful attitudes and actions—and subsequent feelings of guilt—may be at the root of a Christian's depression. Consulting with a trusted counselor often helps victims of depression or burnout define the root causes, make necessary changes in their lives and then move toward recovery.

But doubt, discouragement and depression are also primary weapons used by Satan in the battle against our minds. First he maligns God's character and faithfulness. Then he magnifies the severity of the problem so that we lose sight of God's promises. So while it's important to deal with other possible sources of depression and burnout, it's also crucial to recognize how the enemy operates and to exercise our spiritual muscles in overcoming each condition.

Victory in the Spiritual Realm

James O. Fraser faced such a battle in 1913. He had labored for five years to establish Christian faith among the Lisu tribe in southwest China, with little success. Feeling suicidal, Fraser finally realized the powers of darkness were trying to get rid of him.

Just then—as the rainy season was at its dreariest—a magazine came in the mail. As Fraser read about Christ's triumph over Satan (based on Colossians 2:15), his faith began to rise. He felt he heard the Lord say to him, "Overcome, overcome, even as I also overcame." Fraser wrote to his prayer supporters:

> "Resist the devil" is also Scripture (James 4:7). And I found it worked! That cloud of depression dispersed. I found that I *could* have victory in the spiritual realm whenever I wanted it. The Lord Himself resisted the devil vocally: "Get thee behind me, Satan!" I, in humble dependence on Him, did the same. I talked to Satan at that time, using the promises of Scripture as weapons. And they worked. Right then, the terrible oppression began to pass away. One had to learn, gradually, how to use the newfound weapon of resistance.[2]

Spiritual warriors can learn a valuable lesson from the victory that followed. After he had learned to resist the enemy, Fraser worked successfully for 30 years among the Lisu and saw thousands turn to Christ. The Holy Spirit can help us in the same way: to recognize the source of the attack, to obtain the help of a counselor if need be, and to use the weapon of God's Word to overcome the enemy. The Word not only puts Satan to flight but also brings healing to our troubled souls.

Scriptures

With us is the LORD our God to help us and to fight our battles (2 Chronicles 32:8).

You have made known to me the path of life; you will fill me with joy in your presence, with eternal pleasures at your right hand (Psalm 16:11).

He restores my soul. He guides me in paths of righteousness for his name's sake (Psalm 23:3).

The LORD is my strength and my shield; my heart trusts in him, and I am helped. My heart leaps for joy and I will give thanks to him in song (Psalm 28:7).

I will be glad and rejoice in your love, for you saw my affliction and knew the anguish of my soul (Psalm 31:7).

Restore to me the joy of your salvation and grant me a willing spirit, to sustain me (Psalm 51:12).

Cast your cares on the LORD and he will sustain you; he will never let the righteous fall (Psalm 55:22).

Hear my cry, O God; listen to my prayer. From the ends of the earth I call to you, I call as my heart grows faint; lead me to the rock that is higher than I. For you have been my refuge, a strong tower against the foe. I long to dwell in your tent forever and take refuge in the shelter of your wings (Psalm 61:1-4).

On my bed I remember you; I think of you through the watches of the night. Because you are my help, I sing in the shadow of your wings. My soul clings to you; your right hand upholds me (Psalm 63:6-8).

Praise the LORD, O my soul; all my inmost being, praise his holy name. Praise the LORD, O my soul, and forget not all his benefits—who forgives all your sins and heals all your diseases, who redeems your life from the pit and crowns you with love and compassion, who satisfies your desires with good things so that your youth is renewed like the eagle's (Psalm 103:1-6).

Shouts of joy and victory resound in the tents of the righteous: "The LORD's right hand has done mighty things!" This is the day the LORD has made; let us rejoice and be glad in it (Psalm 118:15,24).

I wait for the LORD, my soul waits, and in his word I put my hope. My soul waits for the Lord more than watchmen wait for the morning. . . . Put your hope in the LORD, for with the LORD is unfailing love and with him is full redemption (Psalm 130:5-7).

You will keep in perfect peace him whose mind is steadfast, because he trusts in you (Isaiah 26:3).

"For I know the plans I have for you," declares the LORD, "plans to prosper you and not to harm you, plans to give you hope and a future" (Jeremiah 29:11).

Yet this I call to mind and therefore I have hope: Because of the LORD's great love we are not consumed, for his compassions never fail. They are new every morning; great is your faithfulness. I say to myself, "The LORD is my portion; therefore I will wait for him." The LORD is good to those whose hope is in him, to the one who seeks him; it is good to wait quietly for the salvation of the LORD (Lamentations 3:21-26).

The LORD your God is with you, he is mighty to save. He will take great delight in you, he will quiet you with his love, he will rejoice over you with singing (Zephaniah 3:17).

Come to me, all you who are weary and burdened, and I will give you rest. Take my yoke upon you and learn from me, for

I am gentle and humble in heart, and you will find rest for your souls. For my yoke is easy and my burden is light (Matthew 11:28-30).

Peace I leave with you; my peace I give you. I do not give to you as the world gives. Do not let your hearts be troubled and do not be afraid (John 14:27).

And we know that in all things God works for the good of those who love him, who have been called according to his purpose.... If God is for us, who can be against us? (Romans 8:28,31).

May the God of hope fill you with all joy and peace as you trust in him, so that you may overflow with hope by the power of the Holy Spirit (Romans 15:13).

Therefore we do not lose heart. Though outwardly we are wasting away, yet inwardly we are being renewed day by day. For our light and momentary troubles are achieving for us an eternal glory that far outweighs them all. So we fix our eyes not on what is seen, but on what is unseen. For what is seen is temporary, but what is unseen is eternal (2 Corinthians 4:16-18).

Do not be anxious about anything, but in everything, by prayer and petition, with thanksgiving, present your requests to God. And the peace of God, which transcends all understanding, will guard your hearts and your minds in Christ Jesus. Finally, brothers, whatever is true, whatever is noble, whatever is right, whatever is pure, whatever is lovely, whatever is admirable—if anything is excellent or praiseworthy—think about such things. Whatever you have learned or received or heard from me, or seen in me—put it into practice. And the God of peace will be with you (Philippians 4:6-9).

Let us fix our eyes on Jesus, the author and perfecter of our faith, who for the joy set before him endured the cross, scorning its shame, and sat down at the right hand of the throne of God (Hebrews 12:2).

Humble yourselves, therefore, under God's mighty hand, that he may lift you up in due time. Cast all your anxiety on him because he cares for you (1 Peter 5:6-7).

Prayer

Lord, thank You that I don't have to live under a cloud of depression. I resist the enemy's attack against my mind, and I choose to put on a garment of praise instead of a spirit of heaviness. Father, I praise You that You are at work even now, restoring the joy of my salvation and restoring my soul in every area. Help me to fix my eyes upon Jesus and not upon my problems. May I find my comfort in You. Amen.

FREEDOM FROM ANXIETY AND FEAR

"Alarm," "fright," "dread," "panic"—all these words describe the same feeling: fear, usually accompanied by its close cousin, anxiety. Many of those who inhabit today's world—including Christian believers—seem plagued by fear. We fear the future, failure, financial loss. We fear being rejected, disapproved, left out, unloved, ignored. We fear disease and death. We fear life itself.

Jesus came to conquer all our fears: "He too shared in their humanity so that by his death he might destroy him who holds the power of death—that is, the devil—and free those who all their lives were held in slavery by their fear of death" (Hebrews 2:14-15).

When God raised Christ from the dead by the power of the Holy Spirit, He proved for time and eternity that Satan is defeated. That same Spirit abides in every person who believes in Jesus as Savior. As Scripture says, "If the Spirit of him who raised Jesus from the dead is living in you, he who raised Christ from the dead will also give life to your mortal bodies through his Spirit, who lives in you" (Romans 8:11).

Knowing that the resurrected Christ dwells in us should eradicate any fear or anxiety stirred up by the enemy. This contemporary song helps us keep the proper perspective:

Every Morning Is Easter Morning
Ev'ry morning is Easter morning from now on!
Ev'ry day's resurrection day, the past is over and gone!
Goodbye guilt, goodbye fear, good riddance!
Hello, Lord, hello, sun! I am one of the Easter People!
My new life has begun!

Ev'ry morning is Easter morning from now on!
Ev'ry day's resurrection day, the past is over and gone!
Daily news is so bad it seems the Good News seldom gets heard.
Get it straight from the Easter People! God's in charge!
Spread the word![1]

Fear Versus Trust

Pastor D. James Kennedy shares a story from the life of Abraham Lincoln that illustrates the futility of fear:

[Lincoln] told of the days when he was a circuit-riding lawyer. He would travel to all the small towns throughout the region, wherever court was being held. This of course involved frequent river crossings, particularly of the notorious Fox River, turbulent and very dangerous in times of heavy rain.

On one occasion, after crossing several rivers with no small amount of difficulty, Lincoln's companion shook his head and said, "If these rivers are this bad, whatever will it be like when we must cross the Fox?"

As it happened, that night they met an itinerant Methodist minister at the inn where they were staying. They asked if he knew the Fox River. "Oh, yes," the preacher said. "I know it well. I have crossed it innumerable times these many long years." They asked if he had any advice about how they might cross it safely.

"Absolutely!" he grinned. "I have discovered a secret about crossing the Fox River which I never fail to keep in mind. It is this: I never cross the Fox River until I *reach* the Fox River. Good night, gentlemen."[2]

Most of the things we fear either never happen or turn out not to be so fearsome after all—a lesson the Methodist minister obviously had learned. Scripture says repeatedly, "Do not be afraid." David's words can become a prayer for us when we feel the threat of fear: "When I am afraid, I will trust in you. In God, whose word I praise, in God I trust; I will not be afraid. What can mortal man do to me?" (Psalm 56:3-4).

Role Models in the Bible

Joshua and Caleb demonstrate a stirring triumph of faith over fear. After God told the Israelites to possess the land across the river Jordan, these two scouts were among those sent by Moses to explore Canaan. All 12 spies agreed it was a wonderful land, just as God had promised. But 10 of the spies were ruled by fear: "We can't attack those people; they are stronger than we are. . . . We seemed like grasshoppers in our own eyes, and we looked the same to them" (Numbers 13:31,33).

Standing against the majority, Joshua and Caleb exhorted the people: "Do not rebel against the LORD. And do not be afraid of the people of the land, because we will swallow them up. Their protection is gone, but the LORD is with us. Do not be afraid of them" (Numbers 14:9). But the Israelites listened to the fearful spies and ignored Joshua and Caleb's appeal. As a consequence, the Israelites spent 40 more years wandering in the wilderness. Nonetheless, God honored the faith of these two spiritual warriors.

When the Israelites did cross over into Canaan, Joshua led them in battle. And God said of Caleb: "But because my servant Caleb has a different spirit and follows me wholeheartedly, I will bring him into the land he went to, and his descendants will inherit it" (Numbers 14:24). God rewards those who faithfully stand on His promises.

Nehemiah offers another example of how to handle fear. As he was directing the rebuilding of the wall of Jerusalem, his enemies ridiculed and threatened him. Nehemiah responded by assigning half the workers to wear their swords while they continued building and the other half to carry additional weapons and stand guard over the workers. Then he told all of the people:

Don't be afraid of them. Remember the Lord, who is great and awesome, and fight for your brothers, your sons and your daughters, your wives and your homes. . . . Wherever you hear the sound of the trumpet, join us there. Our God will fight for us! (Nehemiah 4:14,20).

The enemy repeatedly tried to instill fear in the people and to lure Nehemiah to come down off the wall and talk things over. Nehemiah refused. Later he wrote, "They were all trying to frighten us, thinking,

'Their hands will get too weak for the work, and it will not be completed.' But I prayed, 'Now strengthen my hands'" (Nehemiah 6:9). And God did.

The Israelites finished the work in record time—an example of aggressive faith winning the battle over crippling fear. In our moments of anxiety and fear, we too can declare what God's Word says—even quoting it aloud—and remind the devil that our God will surely fight for us.

Scriptures

Do not be afraid of them; the LORD your God himself will fight for you. But do not be afraid of them; remember well what the LORD your God did to Pharaoh and to all Egypt (Deuteronomy 3:22; 7:18).

When you go to war against your enemies and see horses and chariots and an army greater than yours, do not be afraid of them, because the LORD your God, who brought you up out of Egypt, will be with you (Deuteronomy 20:1).

Be strong and courageous. Do not be afraid or terrified because of them, for the LORD your God goes with you. . . . The LORD himself goes before you and will be with you; he will never leave you nor forsake you. Do not be afraid; do not be discouraged (Deuteronomy 31:6-8).

This is what the LORD says to you: "Do not be afraid or discouraged because of this vast army. For the battle is not yours, but God's." The fear of God came upon all the kingdoms of the countries when they heard how the LORD had fought against the enemies of Israel. And the kingdom of Jehoshaphat was at peace, for his God had given him rest on every side (2 Chronicles 20:15,29-30).

You are a shield around me, O LORD; you bestow glory on me and lift up my head. . . . I will not fear the tens of thousands drawn up against me on every side (Psalm 3:3,6).

Even though I walk through the valley of the shadow of death, I will fear no evil, for you are with me; your rod and your staff, they comfort me (Psalm 23:4).

The LORD is my light and my salvation—whom shall I fear? The LORD is the stronghold of my life—of whom shall I be afraid? When evil men advance against me to devour my flesh, when my enemies and my foes attack me, they will stumble and fall. Though an army besiege me, my heart will not fear; though war break out against me, even then will I be confident (Psalm 27:1-3).

God is our refuge and strength, an ever-present help in trouble. Therefore we will not fear, though the earth give way and the mountains fall into the heart of the sea, though its waters roar and foam and the mountains quake with their surging (Psalm 46:1-3).

Blessed is the man who fears the LORD, who finds great delight in his commands. . . . He will have no fear of bad news; his heart is steadfast, trusting in the LORD. His heart is secure, he will have no fear; in the end he will look in triumph on his foes (Psalm 112:1,7-8).

When you lie down, you will not be afraid; when you lie down, your sleep will be sweet. Have no fear of sudden disaster or of the ruin that overtakes the wicked, for the LORD will be your confidence and will keep your foot from being snared (Proverbs 3:24-26).

So do not fear, for I am with you; do not be dismayed, for I am your God. I will strengthen you and help you; I will uphold you with my righteous right hand. . . . But now, this is what the LORD says—he who created you, O Jacob, he who formed you, O Israel: "Fear not, for I have redeemed you; I have summoned you by name; you are mine" (Isaiah 41:10; 43:1).

"I am the first and I am the last; apart from me there is no God. . . . Do not tremble, do not be afraid. Did I not proclaim this and foretell it long ago? You are my witnesses. Is there any God besides me? No, there is no other Rock; I know not one" (Isaiah 44:6-8).

In righteousness you will be established: Tyranny will be far from you; you will have nothing to fear. Terror will be far removed; it will not come near you (Isaiah 54:14).

This is what the LORD says: "Do not learn the ways of the nations or be terrified by signs in the sky, though the nations are terrified by them. . . . Like a scarecrow in a melon patch, their idols cannot speak; they must be carried because they cannot walk. Do not fear them; they can do no harm nor can they do any good" (Jeremiah 10:2,5).

Blessed is the man who trusts in the LORD, whose confidence is in him. He will be like a tree planted by the water that sends out its roots by the stream. It does not fear when heat comes; its leaves are always green. It has no worries in a year of drought and never fails to bear fruit (Jeremiah 17:7-8).

Do not be afraid, little flock, for your Father has been pleased to give you the kingdom (Luke 12:32).

I have told you these things, so that in me you may have peace. In this world you will have trouble. But take heart! I have overcome the world (John 16:33).

For you did not receive a spirit that makes you a slave again to fear, but you received the Spirit of sonship. And by him we cry, "Abba, Father" (Romans 8:15).

If God is for us, who can be against us? For I am convinced that neither death nor life, neither angels nor demons, neither the present nor the future, nor any powers, neither height nor depth, nor anything else in all creation, will be able to separate us from the love of God that is in Christ Jesus our Lord (Romans 8:31,38-39).

For God did not give us a spirit of timidity, but a spirit of power, of love and of self-discipline (2 Timothy 1:7).

We say with confidence, "The Lord is my helper; I will not be afraid. What can man do to me?" (Hebrews 13:6).

Even if you should suffer for what is right, you are blessed. "Do not fear what they fear; do not be frightened." But in your hearts set apart Christ as Lord. Always be prepared to give an answer to everyone who asks you to give the reason for the hope that you have (1 Peter 3:14-15).

There is no fear in love. But perfect love drives out fear, because fear has to do with punishment. The one who fears is not made perfect in love (1 John 4:18).

Prayer
Father, at those times when I am afraid, let me throw myself upon Your mercy. Give me the confidence of the psalmist who could say he feared no evil, knowing the Shepherd was near. Help me always to remember that because Jesus conquered death, hell and the grave, the enemy has no power to make me afraid. Thank You that Your perfect love casts out all my fears. I put my trust in You, Lord. Amen.

FREEDOM
FROM GUILT

"My guilt has overwhelmed me like a burden too heavy to bear. You know my folly, O God; my guilt is not hidden from you" (Psalms 38:4; 69:5). These words of the psalmist strike a familiar note. We all have experienced remorse over wrong words and wrong actions or felt regret because we failed to speak or act when we should have done so.

We can't go back and play the scene over to get it right, yet we can't seem to shake the guilt. The heavy baggage of our past prevents our moving ahead into the future. Like Adam and Eve, we want to hide from God. Seeking to dull the pain of guilt, many of us find ourselves trapped in destructive addictions.

God, who knows all about guilt, provides the antidote of grace—His unmerited favor. Although we truly deserve punishment for our sins, God sent Jesus into the world to bear the retribution for every sinful person who has ever lived. When we accept His free gift of grace, we are released from the prison of guilt.

In Old Testament times, when a person broke the law and offended God, he brought a lamb as a guilt offering. The priest offered it as a sacrifice to atone for the sin. Long before Christ's birth, Isaiah prophesied that the Messiah Himself would become a guilt offering:

> We all, like sheep, have gone astray, each of us has turned to his own way; and the LORD has laid on him the iniquity of us all. . . . Yet it was the LORD'S will to crush him and cause him to suffer, and though the LORD makes his life a guilt offering, he will see his offspring and prolong his days, and the will of the LORD will prosper in his hand (Isaiah 53:6,10).

When the Holy Spirit convicts us of sin, we must confess it, turn from it and receive God's forgiveness and cleansing. "If we confess our sins, he is faithful and just and will forgive us our sins and purify us from all unrighteousness" (1 John 1:9).

John goes on to proclaim Jesus as the sacrificial lamb for all: "But if anybody does sin, we have one who speaks to the Father in our defense—Jesus Christ, the Righteous One. He is the atoning sacrifice for our sins, and not only for ours but also for the sins of the whole world" (1 John 2:1-2).

To be effective in spiritual warfare, it is essential that we distinguish between true guilt and false guilt. The devil will try every way possible to keep us carrying a load of guilt—whether true or false. Dr. Diane Langberg, a clinical psychologist, discusses this common dilemma:

> True guilt is, of course, that which results from God's judgment, not man's. It is not myself or another who can determine my guilt, but God himself. . . . If the only just judge is God, then I must go to him to decide whether or not I am guilty. . . . There is no simple formula for living a guilt-free life. Nor is there an easy answer for how to determine the validity of the guilt we feel. It involves constantly going back to God and looking at our lives, asking him to sharpen our insights so that we see ourselves more and more clearly.[1]

False guilt is what you feel when you assume the blame for someone else's wrongdoing. Abuse victims often carry such a burden, feeling they surely must have done something wrong to deserve the abuse. But when a victim finally learns to release the burden of false guilt—and to repent for his or her own sin of unforgiveness in the matter—the bondage is broken. In some cases, abuse victims may need the help of a counselor to work through the feelings of guilt and anger until they are able to forgive their abusers and find freedom.

If the devil keeps stirring up guilt—even after you've confessed and repented before the Lord and received His cleansing—you need to vigorously stand against the adversary. You can simply say, "Yes, I did that and it was wrong, but I've asked my heavenly Father to forgive me. Satan, you cannot keep tormenting my mind with that offense. The blood of Jesus covers it. Now be gone, in Jesus' name."

Ed Cole makes this observation about guilt and forgiveness: "Every man must answer for his own actions. And he must answer to God alone. That is why Calvary, where Christ died, is so important. It is the only place in the world where sin can be placed and forgiveness from God received. The only place where guilt can be released."[2]

Scriptures About Confessing Guilt

David was conscience-stricken after he had counted the fighting men, and he said to the LORD, "I have sinned greatly in what I have done. Now, O LORD, I beg you, take away the guilt of your servant. I have done a very foolish thing" (2 Samuel 24:10).

[I] fell on my knees with my hands spread out to the LORD my God and prayed: "O my God, I am too ashamed and disgraced to lift up my face to you, my God, because our sins are higher than our heads and our guilt has reached to the heavens" (Ezra 9:5-6).

I said, "O LORD, have mercy on me; heal me, for I have sinned against you" (Psalm 41:4).

Against you, you only, have I sinned and done what is evil in your sight, so that you are proved right when you speak and justified when you judge. . . . Hide your face from my sins and blot out all my iniquity (Psalm 51:4,9).

We have sinned, even as our fathers did; we have done wrong and acted wickedly (Psalm 106:6).

O LORD, we acknowledge our wickedness and the guilt of our fathers; we have indeed sinned against you (Jeremiah 14:20).

If we claim we have not sinned, we make him out to be a liar and his word has no place in our lives (1 John 1:10).

Scriptures About Removing Guilt

Then hear from heaven, your dwelling place. Forgive and act; deal with each man according to all he does, since you know his heart (for you alone know the hearts of all men) (1 Kings 8:39).

Then I acknowledged my sin to you and did not cover up my iniquity. I said, "I will confess my transgressions to the Lord"— and you forgave the guilt of my sin (Psalm 32:5).

Forgive us our debts, as we also have forgiven our debtors. . . . For if you forgive men when they sin against you, your heavenly Father will also forgive you. But if you do not forgive men their sins, your Father will not forgive your sins (Matthew 6:12,14-15).

And when you stand praying, if you hold anything against any-one, forgive him, so that your Father in heaven may forgive you your sins (Mark 11:25).

When he [the Counselor] comes, he will convict the world of guilt in regard to sin and righteousness and judgment (John 16:8).

It is for freedom that Christ has set us free. Stand firm, then, and do not let yourselves be burdened again by a yoke of slavery. . . . You, my brothers, were called to be free. But do not use your freedom to indulge the sinful nature; rather, serve one another in love (Galatians 5:1,13).

Bear with each other and forgive whatever grievances you may have against one another. Forgive as the Lord forgave you (Colossians 3:13).

Let us draw near to God with a sincere heart in full assurance of faith, having our hearts sprinkled to cleanse us from a guilty conscience and having our bodies washed with pure water (Hebrews 10:22).

Prayer

Thank You, Jesus, for coming to earth to die as a sin offering for me. Thank You that whenever I sin and am burdened by guilt, I need only come to You with true repentance to be cleansed by Your shed blood and restored to fellowship with the Father. What an exchange! What a release! What a gift! Praise You, Lord. Strengthen me to continue to walk in Your freedom and to help set other captives free, in Jesus' name, amen.

OVERCOMING GRIEF
AND DISAPPOINTMENT

Grief is usually associated with the loss of a loved one through death—probably the most traumatic grief experience any of us encounters in life. But we also experience grief and disappointment due to other losses: losing a spouse through divorce, losing friends through broken relationships, losing companionship when friends or children move away, losing a job, losing one's home or valuable possessions, losing one's first love, losing one's hope of achieving a goal.

Any sort of significant loss can throw us into emotional turmoil. Counselor Alfred Ells describes grief as "the natural, unavoidable emotional reaction to loss, a process we emotionally work through until we arrive at a place of acceptance, a place that says, 'I lost and it is okay.'"[1]

Working through such seasons of grief and disappointment inevitably will leave us vulnerable to the attack of the evil one. We need to keep our spiritual radar especially alert during such periods in our lives.

Grieving should follow a natural course over a span of time as the process of healing moves forward. Secular counselors say that this process can last from one to three years or longer, depending on the severity of the loss. A sudden, premature death or a death by suicide or violence is much more traumatic and usually requires even more time to process.

Be aware that unresolved, prolonged grief opens the door to spiritual, physical and emotional problems that can eventually paralyze a person's spiritual progress. To recover, the Christian must go through the same stages of grief as anyone else. However, the more we make use of our spiritual resources, the more we will find the process accelerated. The lows don't have to be as low as for those who grieve with no hope (see 1 Thessalonians 4:13).

Christian counselor H. Dale Wright defines four tasks of grief:

1. Accept your situation rather than deny it. Face the reality of what has happened, even though it opens a floodgate of pain.

2. Allow yourself to feel the pain rather than ignore or repress it. Stifled emotional pain shows up in various ways— such as physical ailments, addictive behavior or irrational anger—and greatly hinders the healing process. Talk about the loss; allow expression of your emotions.

3. Adjust to an environment where that person (or place, job, etc.) is missing. Reorganize your life accordingly. Avoid indulging in self-pity or isolating yourself either physically or emotionally from other believers.

4. Withdraw the emotional energy invested in that person, place or job, and reinvest it in someone or something else. Begin to live life for the present and the future, not in the past.[2]

Christians can and do suffer frustration in their walk with the Lord because they have never properly grieved past losses. Abuse victims, in particular, need to mourn their loss of the innocence of childhood. This time of grieving need not be lengthy, but the loss and sense of betrayal should be acknowledged so that healing can occur.

If you recognize yourself in this scenario, be aware that Satan wants to keep you in a state of spiritual limbo. You can overcome the enemy by asking the Holy Spirit to reveal to you any such unresolved areas of grief, lead you on to healing and then empower you to minister to others with the same needs. Alfred Ells wisely says:

If we embrace our loss and work through the grief with Jesus, we will come to acceptance and resolution. . . . Each loss we suffer is an opportunity to invite Jesus deeper into our lives by

making him our security instead of what we lost. . . . When I
finally cried my tears of loss and profoundly shared with Jesus
my anger, fear, and guilt, I felt his acceptance. At first it felt
strange to mourn something that had happened more than
twenty years ago. But it worked. I felt the self judgment, fear,
and shame dissipate.[3]

Our Lord Jesus knew what it was like to be sorrowful and troubled.
When His friend Lazarus died, "Jesus wept" (John 11:35). He later wept
over the city of Jerusalem (see Matthew 23:37-39). On a dark night in
Gethsemane before His arrest and crucifixion, He asked three close
friends to keep watch with Him because His soul was "overwhelmed
with sorrow to the point of death" (Matthew 26:38).

Because Jesus knew sorrow in His own personal life, He identifies
with us in our grief and disappointment. And when we allow Him to,
He can help us walk through emotional turmoil to victory. Scripture
also offers many words of comfort and healing for the believer who is
working through grief and disappointment.

Scriptures

I am worn out from groaning; all night long I flood my bed with
weeping and drench my couch with tears. . . . The LORD has heard
my cry for mercy; the LORD accepts my prayer (Psalm 6:6,9).

You, O God, do see trouble and grief; you consider it to take it
in hand. The victim commits himself to you; you are the helper
of the fatherless (Psalm 10:14).

Be merciful to me, O LORD, for I am in distress; my eyes grow
weak with sorrow, my soul and my body with grief (Psalm 31:9).

God is our refuge and strength, an ever-present help in trouble
(Psalm 46:1).

From the ends of the earth I call to you, I call as my heart grows
faint; lead me to the rock that is higher than I (Psalm 61:2).

Find rest, O my soul, in God alone; my hope comes from him. He alone is my rock and my salvation; he is my fortress, I will not be shaken. . . . Trust in him at all times, O people; pour out your hearts to him, for God is our refuge (Psalm 62:5-8).

My comfort in my suffering is this: Your promise preserves my life. . . . May your unfailing love be my comfort, according to your promise to your servant (Psalm 119:50,76).

Have no fear of sudden disaster or of the ruin that overtakes the wicked, for the LORD will be your confidence and will keep your foot from being snared (Proverbs 3:25-26).

The Spirit of the Sovereign LORD is on me, because the LORD has . . . sent me to bind up the brokenhearted, to proclaim freedom for the captives . . . and provide for those who grieve in Zion—to bestow on them a crown of beauty instead of ashes, the oil of gladness instead of mourning, and a garment of praise instead of a spirit of despair (Isaiah 61:1-3).

For he [God] does not willingly bring affliction or grief to the children of men (Lamentations 3:33).

Blessed are those who mourn, for they will be comforted (Matthew 5:4).

Praise be to the God and Father of our Lord Jesus Christ, the Father of compassion and the God of all comfort, who comforts us in all our troubles, so that we can comfort those in any trouble with the comfort we ourselves have received from God. For just as the sufferings of Christ flow over into our lives, so also through Christ our comfort overflows. . . . And our hope for you is firm, because we know that just as you share in our sufferings, so also you share in our comfort (2 Corinthians 1:3-7).

One thing I do: Forgetting what is behind and straining toward what is ahead, I press on toward the goal to win the prize for which God has called me heavenward in Christ Jesus (Philippians 3:13-14).

We do not want you to be ignorant about those who fall asleep, or to grieve like the rest of men, who have no hope. We believe that Jesus died and rose again and so we believe that God will bring with Jesus those who have fallen asleep in him. . . . For the Lord himself will come down from heaven, with a loud command, with the voice of the archangel and with the trumpet call of God, and the dead in Christ will rise first (1 Thessalonians 4:13-16).

Let us fix our eyes on Jesus, the author and perfecter of our faith, who for the joy set before him endured the cross, scorning its shame, and sat down at the right hand of the throne of God (Hebrews 12:2).

In this you greatly rejoice, though now for a little while you may have had to suffer grief in all kinds of trials. . . . But you are a chosen people, a royal priesthood, a holy nation, a people belonging to God, that you may declare the praises of him who called you out of darkness into his wonderful light. . . . But rejoice that you participate in the sufferings of Christ, so that you may be overjoyed when his glory is revealed (1 Peter 1:6; 2:9; 4:13).

For the Lamb at the center of the throne will be their shepherd; he will lead them to springs of living water. And God will wipe away every tear from their eyes. . . . There will be no more death or mourning or crying or pain, for the old order of things has passed away (Revelation 7:17; 21:4).

Prayer for the Grieving

Father, I acknowledge to You my pain, anger, fear, sadness, sense of loss and feeling overwhelmed. I place myself in Your hands to be led through this process of grief and sorrow, knowing that You will comfort me and take me at my own pace. Lord, You alone are my refuge—the One who provides total restoration of body, soul and spirit. Thank You for keeping me from being caught in hidden pitfalls of the enemy. I choose to place my trust in You, even though I don't always understand. Surround me with the peace and comfort of Your Holy Spirit, I ask in Jesus' name, amen.

Prayer for the Disappointed

Father, this disappointment is almost more than I can bear, but I rest on Your promise that the Holy Spirit will comfort me. I need the assurance of that comfort now. Thank You that You know the road ahead of me and will order my steps. Help me to trust You in these uncertain times and to walk in the confidence of Your love for me. I refuse to allow the enemy to steal my joy. You alone are my source of life, and I rejoice in You despite my circumstances. Thank You for Your faithfulness, amen.

14

REGAINING SELF-ESTEEM

Though we are made in the image of the Creator God, joint heirs with Christ, many believers continue to suffer from low self-esteem, insecurity and anxiety. Why? Mostly because we lose sight of what a holy heritage we have! Psalm 139 assures us that God knew about each one of us even before our conception:

> O LORD, you have searched me and you know me. You know when I sit and when I rise; you perceive my thoughts from afar. You discern my going out and my lying down; you are familiar with all my ways. For you created my inmost being; you knit me together in my mother's womb. I praise you because I am fearfully and wonderfully made; your works are wonderful, I know that full well (Psalm 139:1-3,13-14).

Often, a person's low self-esteem stems from a background of being rejected or abandoned by those in whom he or she had trusted. Suffering physical, emotional or sexual abuse certainly can result in loss of self-esteem, in which case professional counseling may be necessary. But God's great desire is that we see ourselves as His beloved children. He is a heavenly Father who will never reject or abandon us. Clinical psychologist Diane Langberg writes:

> We may feel useless and inconsequential, of no value to God or others, but how God views us does not depend on how we view ourselves with our own eyes. . . . We have a wrong view of ourselves. Rather than keeping God central, man has put himself in the center.[1]

Dr. Langberg points out how some people invest a great deal of energy in hating themselves, continually focusing on how bad, unimportant and worthless they are. The enemy, who knows our every weakness, constantly reminds us of every failure and shortcoming from the past. Then he plants thoughts of condemnation and a sense of hopelessness that we can never change.

Yet when God sent His Son to die for us, He graphically demonstrated how highly He values us. By sending the Holy Spirit to dwell in our hearts, God again intervened to transform us so that our lives reflect His image. Paul describes this process: "We who with unveiled faces all reflect the Lord's glory, are being transformed into his likeness with ever-increasing glory, which comes from the Lord, who is the Spirit" (2 Corinthians 3:18).

We need to remember that being transformed into God's likeness requires time, just as growing fruit requires time. As a matter of fact, we will not be ripe for the picking until we draw our last breath on this earth! Our encouragement must come from seeing even the smallest steps of growth along the way.

People who suffer low self-esteem are sometimes consumed with anxiety—varying from mild concern to paralyzing dread, or from nagging doubts to excessive brooding. Satan's secret ploy is to assault our minds and emotions, planting ideas that don't line up with God's truth and keeping us focused on our own needs. The mind often proves to be our biggest battleground.

Scripture exhorts us to reject these wrong thoughts and to meditate on God's truth. But since God never violates anyone's free will, we must personally choose to implement these remedies in order to gain victory.

Scriptures for Rejecting Wrong Thoughts

Search me, O God, and know my heart; test me and know my anxious thoughts. See if there is any offensive way in me, and lead me in the way everlasting (Psalm 139:23-24).

Set a guard over my mouth, O LORD; keep watch over the door of my lips. Let not my heart be drawn to what is evil, to take part in wicked deeds with men who are evildoers (Psalm 141:3-4).

Do not conform any longer to the pattern of this world, but be transformed by the renewing of your mind. Then you will be able to test and approve what God's will is—his good, pleasing and perfect will (Romans 12:2).

We demolish arguments and every pretension that sets itself up against the knowledge of God, and we take captive every thought to make it obedient to Christ (2 Corinthians 10:5).

You were taught, with regard to your former way of life, to put off your old self, which is being corrupted by its deceitful desires; to be made new in the attitude of your minds; and to put on the new self, created to be like God in true righteousness and holiness (Ephesians 4:22-24).

I have often told you before and now say again even with tears, many live as enemies of the cross of Christ. . . . Their mind is on earthly things. But our citizenship is in heaven. And we eagerly await a Savior from there, the Lord Jesus Christ, who, by the power that enables him to bring everything under his control, will transform our lowly bodies so that they will be like his glorious body (Philippians 3:18-21).

Scriptures on Meditating on God's Word

Do not let this Book of the Law depart from your mouth; meditate on it day and night, so that you may be careful to do everything written in it. Then you will be prosperous and successful (Joshua 1:8).

And you, my son Solomon, acknowledge the God of your father, and serve him with wholehearted devotion and with a willing mind, for the LORD searches every heart and understands every motive behind the thoughts. If you seek him, he will be found by you; but if you forsake him, he will reject you forever (1 Chronicles 28:9).

I will meditate on all your works and consider all your mighty deeds (Psalm 77:12).

"Love the Lord your God with all your heart and with all your soul and with all your mind." This is the first and greatest commandment (Matthew 22:37-38).

We have the mind of Christ (1 Corinthians 2:16).

If anyone is in Christ, he is a new creation; the old has gone, the new has come! (2 Corinthians 5:17).

Other Scriptures

Job replied to the LORD: "I know that you can do all things; no plan of yours can be thwarted" (Job 42:1-2).

The LORD will fulfill his purpose for me (Psalm 138:8).

My frame was not hidden from you when I was made in the secret place. When I was woven together in the depths of the earth, your eyes saw my unformed body. All the days ordained for me were written in your book before one of them came to be. How precious to me are your thoughts, O God! How vast is the sum of them! Were I to count them, they would outnumber the grains of sand. When I awake, I am still with you (Psalm 139:15-18).

The tongue has the power of life and death (Proverbs 18:21).

Many are the plans in a man's heart, but it is the LORD's purpose that prevails (Proverbs 19:21).

Forget the former things; do not dwell on the past. See, I am doing a new thing! Now it springs up; do you not perceive it? (Isaiah 43:18-19).

If God is for us, who can be against us? (Romans 8:31).

Because of his great love for us, God, who is rich in mercy, made us alive with Christ even when we were dead in transgressions. . . . And God raised us up with Christ and seated us with him in the heavenly realms in Christ Jesus. For we are God's workmanship, created in Christ Jesus to do good works, which God prepared in advance for us to do (Ephesians 2:4-6,10).

I [Paul] was shown mercy so that in me, the worst of sinners, Christ Jesus might display his unlimited patience as an example for those who would believe on him and receive eternal life (1 Timothy 1:16).

God is love. Whoever lives in love lives in God, and God in him (1 John 4:16).

Prayer

Lord, I am forever grateful that You lifted me out of despair and put my feet on solid ground. Thank You for loving me enough to die for me—even when I was unlovable. Help me always to yield to Your plan as You conform me to Your own image. I know that if You are for me—and You are—then no plan of the enemy will succeed. Lord, help me to live so that others will see Your beauty in me. In Jesus' name, amen.

PART III

DEFENDING THE HOME FRONT

15

WARFARE FOR YOUR MARRIAGE AND BROKEN RELATIONSHIPS

Perhaps you consider that your marriage has been reasonably healthy most of the time over the years since your wedding day. You and your spouse are both Christians, you're usually compatible, and you share fairly common goals. Yet you can see yourself in one or more of the following scenarios. In fact, you may even be deeply concerned about how often one of these incidents takes place:

- Bickering with your mate over relatively minor matters and then holding a grudge afterwards

- Feeling resentment when your spouse spends money without first discussing it with you

- Feeling neglected when you are home alone while your spouse is at a meeting in which you are not included, or while your spouse is spending time with people you feel are a negative influence on him or her

- Finding yourself saying or hearing "Why are you always late?" (or some other negative "always" or "never" expression)

- Feeling resentment when your spouse is more polite or attentive to others (especially of the opposite sex) than to you

- Thinking your spouse is sure to misunderstand if you try to express your true feelings—so you stifle them

- Measuring the amount of time that has passed since the last compliment, "I love you" gift or romantic experience

- Realizing that you have been comparing your companion un-
  favorably with a current acquaintance or former sweetheart

- Finding yourself wanting to conceal from your partner certain friendships, purchases or ways you spend your time

- Wishing your partner were as spiritual (or as friendly, or as
  interesting) as you feel yourself to be or as someone else
  whom you admire

These vignettes are examples of nitty-gritty problems with which
many Christian partners struggle. If not confronted and dealt with
through prayer, asking for and granting forgiveness and/or seeking
godly counsel, such seemingly small problems may end up damaging
a relationship. They are footholds the devil will exploit in an effort to
destroy a marriage (see Ephesians 4:26-27).

Following God's Plan

Marriage, family and home were God's plan from the beginning of
creation. The second chapter of Genesis records God's words after He
had created Adam: "It is not good for the man to be alone. I will make
a helper suitable for him" (Genesis 2:18). When God formed a woman
from the rib He had taken out of the man, Adam expressed great delight. "God blessed them and said to them, 'Be fruitful and increase in
number; fill the earth and subdue it' " (Genesis 1:28).

Because marriage was instigated by God, Satan does anything and
everything possible to tear it down. He tries to damage relationships
between righteous people by bringing division and misunderstand-
ing, which can lead to resentment, estrangement or divorce.

Protecting Your Marriage

Paul teaches that God intended marriage to be a picture of the relationship between Christ and His church (see Ephesians 5:21-24). Is it
any wonder that Satan lashes out at marriages, trying to destroy them?
Or that he tries to ravage the fruit of marriage, our children? God
wants us to be aware of Satan's schemes and to guard against them
(see 2 Corinthians 2:11; Ephesians 6:11).

Christian couples who want their marriages to thrive make it a priority to pray together, to walk in mutual forgiveness and to keep their communication with one another open and honest. Dr. Archibald Hart writes:

> If we are married, we need to focus on our marriage relationship. Since our relationship with our spouse is to be our sole sexual focus, this is where we need to direct our attention. Building a good marriage is hard work. Every marriage begins with the union of two incompatible people in an impossible relationship. The task God gives us in marriage is to turn it into something beautiful. With God's grace—it *can* be done.[1]

In God's design, the couple's sexual union causes them to "become one flesh" (Ephesians 5:31)—meaning the two are bonded or cemented together. Concerning sexual relationships outside of marriage, Paul writes:

> Do you not know that he who unites himself with a prostitute is one with her in body? For it is said, "The two will become one flesh." Flee from sexual immorality. . . . He who sins sexually sins against his own body (1 Corinthians 6:16,18).

The author of the letter of Hebrews puts it this way: "Marriage should be honored by all, and the marriage bed kept pure, for God will judge the adulterer and all the sexually immoral" (Hebrews 13:4). Clearly, God desires that marriage partners be faithful to one another sexually. To protect themselves from attack in this area, wise believers know they must work at keeping the relationship strong, both spiritually and emotionally.

Praying for an Unfaithful Partner

While there is no *formula* for praying for an unfaithful partner, there are biblical examples that point us to powerful prayer strategies. One story tells of how God intervened on behalf of Hosea, a husband with a straying wife:

She [Gomer] said, "I will go after my lovers, who give me my food and my water, my wool and my linen, my oil and my drink." Therefore I [God] will block her path with thorn-bushes; I will wall her in so that she cannot find her way. She will chase after her lovers but not catch them; she will look for them but not find them. Then she will say, "I will go back to my husband as at first for then I was better off than now" (Hosea 2:5-7).

God told Hosea he would block Gomer's path with thorns, so her lovers would lose interest in her. That's exactly what happened. God hedged her in and kept Gomer and her lovers from finding one another. That protective barrier resulted in Gomer's change of heart.

Hosea's story can serve as a pattern for those praying for unfaithful partners or for those praying for anyone in an adulterous relationship. No person can overcome a spouse's willful determination to pursue an adulterous affair. But we can ask God to intervene as only He is able. Pray that the Lord would arrest that person's attention, provide a barrier between the straying spouse and his or her lover, and place a strong believer in the wayward person's path to speak God's Word into the situation.

Repairing a Broken Relationship

It is essential that an unfaithful partner who returns to his or her spouse break the unholy bonds established through any illicit sexual relationships. In order to do this, the returning spouse should do the following:

1. Repent for breaking God's law. Ask God's forgiveness for each liaison, mentioning in prayer the names of those with whom you had sexual relationships outside marriage.

2. Declare in the name of Jesus that all past bondings are now broken and will no longer affect you.

3. Command all unclean spirits associated with past illicit relationships to leave you in the name of Jesus. The devil

has no more rights in that area of your life because it is under the blood of Jesus.

4. Thank God for His forgiveness, His cleansing, and for your marriage partner who took you back.

5. Ask the Lord to strengthen you to walk in your freedom, and "not be entangled again with a yoke of bondage" (Galatians 5:1, *NKJV*).[2]

Forgiving to Bring Freedom

Some families are constantly plagued by strife, anger, bitterness or tension because one or more family members has opened a door to the enemy. Such divisiveness is often due to a person's own willful disobedience, rebellion, jealousy, immorality, involvement with the occult, idolatry, pride, selfishness or substance abuse—to name only a few possible culprits.

The enemy seizes any available foothold to gain access to our closest relationships. If your family exhibits any specific pattern of sin (such as adultery, incest, addiction or occult involvement), you may need to break its power in prayer. Before he returned to Jerusalem to rebuild the demolished wall of his ancestors' homeland, Nehemiah wept, mourned, fasted, prayed and confessed the sins of his forefathers (see Nehemiah 1:6-7).

While we cannot force an adult to give up his or her choice to sin, we can prevent another person's disobedience from ruining our relationship with the Lord (and others) and robbing us of joy. The key factor in restoring any broken relationship is *forgiveness.*

No freedom can compare to that which comes when we decide to forgive anyone against whom we have held a grudge because he or she hurt us in some way. This releases the other person from our judgment and also sets us free from the poisonous sin of unforgiveness. That release allows God to deal more directly with the offender without interference.

One Bible teacher declared, "To forgive is like acquitting a defendant, clearing him even if he's guilty, and dealing with him as though innocent. It is freeing one, as it were, from prison, chains or bondage." Forgiveness carries a connected promise, as these verses illustrate:

Do not judge, and you will not be judged. Do not condemn, and you will not be condemned. Forgive, and you will be forgiven (Luke 6:37).

Speak and act as those who are going to be judged by the law that gives freedom, because judgment without mercy will be shown to anyone who has not been merciful. Mercy triumphs over judgment! (James 2:12-13).

Jesus died to cancel our huge debt of sin. If the Son of God could hang on a cross and say, "Father, forgive them," how can we not forgive the one who has wounded us? Ask the Lord to help you to make that choice. Forgiveness is an *act of the will,* not an *emotion.* When you choose to follow the example of Christ, He quickly comes to your aid.

Forgiveness also can be defined as unconditionally bestowing or granting our favor, or laying down our desire to get even. We see this perspective modeled in Paul's letter to the Ephesians: "Get rid of all bitterness, rage and anger, brawling and slander, along with every form of malice. Be kind and compassionate to one another, forgiving each other, just as in Christ God forgave you" (Ephesians 4:31-32).

After forgiveness has been freely bestowed, you and your spouse may need the help of a qualified counselor to restore your communication and rebuild trust. Unfortunately, some marriages do fail when both parties are not willing to work toward reconciliation. (For a fuller discussion about praying for marriages, see our book *A Woman's Guide to Spiritual Warfare.*)

Many women find themselves in a divorce situation through no fault of their own, and sadly, they may have been made to feel like second-class citizens. But God sees their hearts, knows their shame and comforts them in their new role of singleness. Even in a worst-case scenario, God can strengthen and sustain you no matter what course of action your spouse may choose.

Prayer for Breaking a Sin Pattern

Father God, I confess before You the sins of my ancestors and ask You to have mercy on me and all members of my family. Forgive us for the sin of [name the sin] that has been in our family for generations.

Thank You that Jesus Christ came to set us free from the curse of the iniquities of our forefathers. I pray that each member of my family will receive the cleansing of the blood of Jesus and the deliverance He alone can give. By the power and authority of Jesus Christ, I destroy that sin pattern and declare its curse broken. It has no more right to invade our family line. Thank You, Father, for the freedom that is ours through the shed blood of Your Son, Jesus Christ! Amen.

Scriptures on Marriage

Unless the LORD builds the house, its builders labor in vain (Psalm 127:1).

He who finds a wife finds what is good and receives favor from the LORD (Proverbs 18:22).

A wife of noble character who can find? She is worth far more than rubies. Her children arise and call her blessed; her husband also, and he praises her: "Many women do noble things, but you surpass them all" (Proverbs 31:10,28-29).

The LORD is acting as the witness between you and the wife of your youth, because you have broken faith with her, though she is your partner, the wife of your marriage covenant. Has not [the LORD] made them one? In flesh and spirit they are his. And why one? Because he was seeking godly offspring. So guard yourself in your spirit, and do not break faith with the wife of your youth (Malachi 2:14-15).

The Lord, the God of Israel, says: I hate divorce and marital separation and him who covers his garment [his wife] with violence. Therefore keep a watch upon your spirit [that it may be controlled by My Spirit], that you deal not treacherously and faithlessly [with your marriage mate] (Malachi 2:16, *AMP*).

For this reason a man will leave his father and mother and be united to his wife, and the two will become one flesh. So they are no longer two, but one. Therefore what God has joined together, let man not separate (Mark 10:7-9).

The husband should fulfill his marital duty to his wife, and likewise the wife to her husband. The wife's body does not belong to her alone but also to her husband. In the same way, the husband's body does not belong to him alone but also to his wife (1 Corinthians 7:3-4).

A woman is bound to her husband as long as he lives. But if her husband dies, she is free to marry anyone she wishes, but he must belong to the Lord (1 Corinthians 7:39).

Love is patient, love is kind. It does not envy, it does not boast, it is not proud. It is not rude, it is not self-seeking, it is not easily angered, it keeps no record of wrongs. Love does not delight in evil but rejoices with the truth. It always protects, always trusts, always hopes, always perseveres (1 Corinthians 13:4-7).

Wives, submit to your husbands as to the Lord. For the husband is the head of the wife as Christ is the head of the church, his body, of which he is the Savior. Now as the church submits to Christ, so also wives should submit to their husbands in everything. Husbands, love your wives, just as Christ loved the church and gave himself up for her. In this same way, husbands ought to love their wives as their own bodies. He who loves his wife loves himself (Ephesians 5:22-25,28).

Husbands . . . be considerate as you live with your wives, and treat them with respect as the weaker partner and as heirs with you of the gracious gift of life, so that nothing will hinder your prayers (1 Peter 3:7).

Prayer for Wives to Pray

Lord, I desire to be the mate for my husband that You want me to be and that he needs. Enable me to be a help and encouragement to him

all the days of his life, and may he always have confidence in me.
Strengthen me to watch over the affairs of our household wisely.
Lord, help us to mutually respect and love one another.
May our home be a place of peace and security where we honor
and worship You, I ask in Jesus' name, amen.

Prayer for Husbands to Pray

Lord, may I love my wife as Jesus loved the Church. I thank You
for this special woman You have provided for me. Help me to show
her how much I love, appreciate and cherish her. May I be a faithful
partner and good provider for her. Help us to serve You together,
Father, and to be a godly example to our children,
I ask in Jesus' name, amen.

Scripture Prayer for a Believing Spouse

Father, I pray that You, the God of peace, will sanctify my
husband/wife through and through—making him/her pure and
wholly consecrated to You. May his/her spirit, soul and body be
preserved sound and complete and be found blameless at the coming
of our Lord Jesus Christ. Father, I know that You—the One
who has called him/her—are faithful and utterly trustworthy,
and will do it [see 1 Thessalonians 5:23-24, AMP].

Scripture Prayer for an Unbelieving Spouse

Lord, I pray that You will open the eyes of my unbelieving
husband/wife and turn him/her from darkness to light and from the
power of Satan to God so that he/she may receive forgiveness of sins
and a place among those who are sanctified by faith in Jesus Christ.
Father, please send someone across his/her path who
will gently instruct him/her, in the hope that God will grant
him/her repentance leading to a knowledge of the truth and
that he/she will come to his/her senses and escape from the trap
of the devil, who has taken him/her captive to do his will
[see Acts 26:18 and 2 Timothy 2:25-26].

Scriptures on Strife

Set a guard over my mouth, O LORD; keep watch over the door of my lips (Psalm 141:3).

Above all else, guard your heart, for it is the wellspring of life. Put away perversity from your mouth; keep corrupt talk far from your lips (Proverbs 4:23-24).

A gentle answer turns away wrath, but a harsh word stirs up anger. He who guards his mouth and his tongue keeps himself from calamity (Proverbs 15:1; 21:23).

By your words you will be acquitted, and by your words you will be condemned (Matthew 12:37).

If it is possible, as far as it depends on you, live at peace with everyone (Romans 12:18).

Do nothing out of selfish ambition or vain conceit, but in humility consider others better than yourselves. Each of you should look not only to your own interests, but also to the interests of others. Your attitude should be the same as that of Christ Jesus (Philippians 2:3-5).

My dear brothers, take note of this: Everyone should be quick to listen, slow to speak and slow to become angry (James 1:19).

Prayer Against Strife

Lord, give me the wisdom to help repair breaches and mend broken relationships. May I not be a party to strife and dissension. I want to be pleasing to You, as well as a good example to others, especially to my spouse and family members. Keep my mouth from deceit and malice. Help me, with the strength only You can provide, to walk in forgiveness, in Jesus' name, amen.

STANDING FOR YOUR CHILDREN

Children are a priceless gift, a heritage from the Lord. What a privilege to stand in the gap for them, praying that they will achieve God's full potential.

God has cared deeply about families since He first brought Adam and Eve together. When He destroyed the earth with a flood because of humanity's wickedness, He chose to spare Noah and his family. Just as their salvation hinged upon their entering the door of the ark, so our families have one door of entrance to salvation: Jesus Christ.

As parents, we resonate with Joshua's cry: "But as for me and my household, we will serve the LORD" (Joshua 24:15). Even if you are not a parent, God may want you to stand in the prayer gap for children—perhaps those who have no one interceding for them. Children in need of a Savior are everywhere—in schools, churches, neighborhoods, streets, subways, buses, shopping malls, beaches, parks. But your love and prayers can make a difference.

Personalizing Scripture

One especially effective spiritual warfare tactic involves personalizing verses of Scripture as you pray. Usually, this is as easy as replacing the scriptural pronouns with the names of the children or people for whom you are interceding. For example, Psalm 23:3 could be personalized in this way: *"Thank You, Lord, that You guide my son [name] in the paths of righteousness for your name's sake."* The verse takes on added potency as both an expression of praise to the Lord and a declaration of truth to the enemy.

We pray differently for children during various phases of their lives. For instance, the following is a combination of paraphrased verses to pray for a child who is either a student or an employee:

Lord, may my child, like Daniel, show aptitude for every kind of learning and be well informed, quick to understand and qualified to serve in places of influence and authority. May he/she speak with wisdom and tact and be found to have a keen mind, knowledge and understanding and also the ability to solve difficult problems. Lord, I pray You will endow [name] with wisdom and great insight and a breadth of understanding as measureless as the sand on the seashore [see Daniel 1:4; 2:14; 5:12 and 1 Kings 4:29].

Another way to personalize these same Scripture verses would be to substitute your child's name for the pronouns shown and declare them aloud: *"My child will exhibit an attitude for every kind of learning, be well informed and quick to understand. He/she will speak with wisdom and tact. He/she will be found to have a keen mind and knowledge and understanding and the ability to solve difficult problems. He/she does have wisdom and insight and breadth of understanding as measureless as the sand on the seashore."*

By hearing the Word of God—even from our own lips—we stand firm on His truth and apply it to our very own family. Not only have we strengthened our personal faith, but we have also delivered a blow to the kingdom of darkness.

Personalized Scripture Prayers
Concerning Spiritual Growth

Thank You, Lord, that You know the plans You have for my child, plans to prosper [name] and not to harm [him/her], plans to give [name] a hope and a future [see Jeremiah 29:11].

May my child live a life worthy of the Lord and please You in every way: bearing fruit in every good work, growing in the knowledge of God, being strengthened with all power according to Your glorious might so that [name] may have great endurance and patience, and joyfully give thanks to the Father, who has qualified [him/her] to share in the inheritance of the saints in the kingdom of light. For he has rescued [name] from the dominion of darkness and brought [him/her] into the kingdom of the Son He loves, in whom [name] has redemption, the forgiveness of sins [see Colossians 1:10-14].

Drawing Up Battle Plans

All children, be they wayward or godly, need prayer. But the types of prayers will differ according to specific circumstances. Biblical battles were not all fought with the same strategy. Similarly, we seek *God's battle plan* when praying for our children, asking Him to reveal appropriate Scriptures for each situation. Let's consider how God may lead you to pray for a child who is being adversely influenced by peers:

1. Pray as David did when he believed his son Absalom was hearing the wrong advice. Ask the Lord to turn into foolishness the counsel your child is receiving (see 2 Samuel 15:31).

2. Pray that your child be delivered from wicked and evil men, and that God would strengthen and protect him/her from the evil one (see 2 Thessalonians 3:2-3).

3. Bless each peer, even when your natural inclination is to ask God to remove that harmful influence from your child's life. You can pray that God will accomplish His plan and purpose in that person, bringing the right people into his or her life at the right time (see Ephesians 1:11; Matthew 9:38). God broke Job's captivity when he prayed for his friends, and they weren't exactly the kind of friends most of us would want (see Job 42:10).

Ask God to lead you to other Scriptures to pray, some listed in this chapter.

Godly Goals

What does God desire for our children? His Word provides many answers concerning the heart of our heavenly Father toward his little ones:

1. That Jesus Christ be formed in them (see Galatians 4:19)

2. That they—the seed of the righteous—will be delivered from the evil one (see Proverbs 11:21; Matthew 6:13)

3. That they "will be taught by the LORD" and their peace will be great (Isaiah 54:13)

4. That they will train themselves to discern good from evil (see Hebrews 5:14) and have "a good conscience toward God" (1 Peter 3:21)

5. That God's laws will be in their minds and on their hearts (see Hebrews 8:10)

6. That they will choose companions who are wise—not fools or those who are sexually immoral, drunkards, idolaters, slanderers or swindlers (see Proverbs 13:20; 1 Corinthians 5:11)

7. That they will remain sexually pure and keep themselves only for their spouse, asking God for His grace to keep such a commitment (see Ephesians 5:3,31-33)

8. That they will honor their parents (Ephesians 6:1-3)

Many other Scriptures could be added to this list, which will change over time as God shows you new ways to pray His Word. Ask Him for specific promises to stand on during difficult situations.

Scriptures About Children

Know therefore that the LORD your God is God; he is the faithful God, keeping his covenant of love to a thousand generations of those who love him and keep his commands (Deuteronomy 7:9).

Remember the Lord, who is great and awesome, and fight for your brothers, your sons and your daughters, your wives and your homes (Nehemiah 4:14).

Sons are a heritage from the LORD, children a reward from him (Psalm 127:3).

Train a child in the way he should go, and when he is old he will not turn from it (Proverbs 22:6).

Do not be afraid, for I am with you; I will bring your children
from the east and gather you from the west.... For I will pour
water on the thirsty land, and streams on the dry ground; I
will pour out my Spirit on your offspring, and my blessing on
your descendants (Isaiah 43:5; 44:3).

This is what the LORD says: "I will contend with those who
contend with you, and your children I will save" (Isaiah 49:25).

All your sons will be taught by the LORD, and great will be your
children's peace. No weapon forged against you will prevail,
and you will refute every tongue that accuses you. This is the
heritage of the servants of the LORD, and this is their vindication from me," declares the LORD (Isaiah 54:13,17).

"As for me, this is my covenant with them," says the LORD.
"My Spirit, who is on you, and my words that I have put in
your mouth will not depart from your mouth, or from the
mouths of your children, or from the mouths of their descendants from this time on and forever," says the LORD (Isaiah 59:21).

This is what the LORD says: "Restrain your voice from weeping
and your eyes from tears, for your work will be rewarded," declares the LORD. They will return from the land of the enemy.
So there is hope for your future," declares the LORD. "Your
children will return to their own land" (Jeremiah 31:16-17).

I will pour out my Spirit on all people. Your sons and daughters will prophesy (Joel 2:28).

He will turn the hearts of the fathers to their children, and
the hearts of the children to their fathers (Malachi 4:6).

The promise [of the Holy Spirit] is for you and your children
and for all who are far off—for all whom the Lord our God
will call (Acts 2:39).

I have not stopped giving thanks for you, remembering you in my prayers. I keep asking that the God of our Lord Jesus Christ, the glorious Father, may give you the Spirit of wisdom and revelation, so that you may know him better. I pray also that the eyes of your heart may be enlightened in order that you may know the hope to which he has called you, the riches of his glorious inheritance in the saints, and his incomparably great power (Ephesians 1:16-19).

I pray that out of his glorious riches he may strengthen you with power through his Spirit in your inner being, so that Christ may dwell in your hearts through faith. And I pray that you, being rooted and established in love, may have power . . . to grasp how wide and long and high and deep is the love of Christ, and to know this love that surpasses knowledge—that you may be filled to the measure of all the fullness of God (Ephesians 3:16-19).

Scriptures for Salvation

Surely the arm of the LORD is not too short to save, nor his ear too dull to hear (Isaiah 59:1).

Believe in the Lord Jesus, and you will be saved—you and your household (Acts 16:31).

I am sending you to them to open their eyes and turn them from darkness to light, and from the power of Satan to God, so that they may receive forgiveness of sins and a place among those who are sanctified by faith in me [Jesus] (Acts 26:17-18).

Do you show contempt for the riches of his kindness, tolerance and patience, not realizing that God's kindness leads you toward repentance? (Romans 2:4).

God our Savior . . . wants all men to be saved and to come to a knowledge of the truth (1 Timothy 2:3-4).

The Lord is not slow in keeping his promise, as some under-stand slowness. He is patient with you, not wanting anyone to perish, but everyone to come to repentance (2 Peter 3:9).

A Declaration of Faith
Addressed to the Enemy

Devil, the Word of God says you have held my child captive to do your will. In the name of Jesus Christ, the Lord to whom I belong, I bind your power and tell you to release the will of [child's name], leaving him/her free to choose Jesus and God's plan for his/her life. Jesus' blood was shed for him/her. My child will come to his/her senses and escape from your trap. His/Her eyes will be opened and he/she will turn from darkness to light, translated from Satan's kingdom to God's kingdom. [Name] will receive forgiveness of sins and a place among those sanctified in the Lord Jesus. I believe in the Lord Jesus, and my household shall be saved.

Prayer for Our Children

Thank You, Lord, that You will contend with those who contend with me, and You will save my children. I claim Your promise that You will bring back from the land of the enemy those who have strayed. I rejoice that You overshadow them with Your protection and that You will fulfill Your promises for them. Thank You, Lord, for the gift of these precious children. Amen.

STANDING AGAINST CHILDLESSNESS OR ABORTION

"Be fruitful and multiply," the Lord commanded Adam and Eve. When a couple becomes one in flesh and spirit through marriage, God normally intends for them to produce godly offspring (see Genesis 1:28; Malachi 2:15).

Married men and women usually experience a God-given desire to have children together. But sometimes pregnancy does not happen as easily as they had hoped. Infertility actually afflicts about 15 percent of couples and may result from either the man or the woman—or both—being incapable of reproduction. Doctors may be able to help, but God, the author of life, is ever ready to hear our cry of need.

Perhaps no other woman cried out so much for a baby as did Hannah. God eventually gave her and her husband many children after she had given her firstborn, Samuel, to the Lord. Samuel later became a great prophet of God. In the biblical examples of God's intervention on behalf of childless couples, we can make three observations:

1. God gave the couple a child as a promise.
2. God answered the prayers of the wife or husband.
3. God gave the couple children because it was His intention for them to have a family.

Today God is still performing miracles to give children to couples struggling with infertility.

Specifically praying for God to help you conceive a child acknowledges the Creator as the source of life as well as the One to praise and honor when the birth occurs. Satan, on the other hand, does everything he can to frustrate conception, thus eliminating potential godly offspring. Satan often perverts sex, plants unbelief and fear, and scrambles communication between spouses to bring division and strife.

Having difficulty conceiving can sometimes be more spiritual in nature. All of us are warned not to bring false gods or occult objects into our homes, as we could subject ourselves to a curse (see Deuteronomy 27-28 and other teachings on the occult in chapter 20 of this book). As a couple, ask the Holy Spirit to reveal to you whether this is an issue needing to be addressed. If so, you should destroy all such objects, repent of the forbidden acts and renounce any curse or ties with occult activity. Then accept the Lord's forgiveness and thank Him that "Christ redeemed us from the curse of the law by becoming a curse for us" (Galatians 3:13).

A suggested declaration: "Father God, we renounce all ties and association with occult practices and the works of darkness, and declare that they have no power over us. We submit ourselves to the Lordship of Jesus Christ, and we apply the blood of Jesus to our lives, our marriage relationship and our home."

Don't let the enemy directly or through other people inflict guilt or condemnation upon you if you have been unable to produce children. God can use your talents and love for His little ones in many creative ways. When a married couple yearns for a child, what encouragement they gain by reading aloud God's Word as they stand in faith for a baby.

Scriptures for Fruitfulness

Now the LORD was gracious to Sarah as he had said, and the LORD did for Sarah what he had promised. Sarah became pregnant and bore a son to Abraham in his old age, at the very time God had promised him (Genesis 21:1-2).

Isaac prayed to the LORD on behalf of his wife, because she was barren. The LORD answered his prayer, and his wife Rebekah became pregnant (Genesis 25:21).

Worship the LORD your God, and his blessing will be on your food and water. I will take away sickness from among you, and none will miscarry or be barren in your land. I will give you a full life span (Exodus 23:25).

So Boaz took Ruth and she became his wife. . . . And the LORD enabled her to conceive, and she gave birth to a son. The women said to Naomi: "Praise be to the LORD, who this day has not left you without a kinsman-redeemer. May he become famous throughout Israel! He will renew your life and sustain you in your old age. For your daughter-in-law, who loves you and who is better to you than seven sons, has given him birth" (Ruth 4:13-15).

In bitterness of soul Hannah wept much and prayed to the LORD. And she made a vow, saying, "O LORD Almighty, if you will only look upon your servant's misery and remember me, and not forget your servant but give her a son, then I will give him to the LORD for all the days of his life, and no razor will ever be used on his head. . . . I prayed for this child, and the LORD has granted me what I asked of him. So now I give him to the LORD. For his whole life he will be given over to the LORD" (1 Samuel 1:10-11,27-28).

He settles the barren woman in her home as a happy mother of children. Praise the LORD (Psalm 113:9).

Blessed are all who fear the LORD, who walk in his ways. . . . Your wife will be like a fruitful vine within your house; your sons will be like olive shoots around your table (Psalm 128:1-3).

I am the LORD, the God of all mankind. Is anything too hard for me? (Jeremiah 32:27).

Then an angel of the Lord appeared to him. . . . "Do not be afraid, Zechariah; your prayer has been heard. Your wife Elizabeth will bear you a son, and you are to give him the name John. He will be a joy and delight to you, and many will rejoice because of his birth, for he will be great in the sight of the Lord."

After this his wife Elizabeth became pregnant and for five months remained in seclusion. "The Lord has done this for me," she said. "In these days he has shown his favor and taken away my disgrace among the people" (Luke 1:11-15,24-25).

Now to him who is able to do immeasurably more than all we ask or imagine, according to his power that is at work within us, to him be glory in the church and in Christ Jesus throughout all generations, for ever and ever! Amen (Ephesians 3:20-21).

Prayer to Have a Child

Father God, Creator of life, we come to You with our great desire to have children. We know through Your Word that You have a special love for children, and that Jesus took time to bless the little ones who came to Him. Lord, we ask that You answer our hearts' cry for a child, whether by birth or by adoption. We submit our wills to You and trust Your great plan and purpose for our lives. Father, may Your peace and Your presence sustain us as we wait upon You, in Jesus' name, amen.

A Spirit of Murder

Because life is so precious to God, who created life, He is grieved over abortion, or murder in the womb. Jesus Himself says the devil was a murderer from the beginning (see John 8:44). The Family Research Council website carries this statement:

> Few things touch on the sanctity of human life more than the practice of abortion. A pregnancy should not simply be "terminated," as if it were something impersonal and problematic, and it cannot be without physical and emotional consequences. A child in the womb is a distinct, developing, wholly human being, and each time a mother decides or a father pressures to end such a life, it is a profound tragedy. Abortion harms the mother as well, and deprives society of the gifts of the unborn. [1]

Consider these facts: Human beings develop at an astonishingly rapid pace. The cardiovascular system is the first major system to function. The blood is circulating and the heart begins to beat about 21 or 22 days (3 weeks) after conception, and can be detected by ultrasound.[2] By the end of the eighth week, the unborn child has developed all its organs and biological systems.[3]

Besides depriving life to the child, abortion causes serious problems for the woman who makes this choice. The following are just a few statistics about post-abortive women that reinforce this truth:

- 44 percent reported nervous disorders.
- 36 percent reported sleep disturbances.
- 31 percent expressed regrets for their decision.
- 28 percent had attempted suicide.
- 25 percent had sought psychiatric counseling, compared to 3 percent of the control group.
- 19 percent suffered from post traumatic stress syndrome.
- 11 percent had had psychotropic drugs prescribed by doctors.[4]

Even though abortion is legal in our nation, the fact remains that the woman who chooses abortion is voluntarily depriving a child from being born, which equates with murder. God has a higher standard, which should supersede an individual's choice: "Let no one be found among you who sacrifices his son or daughter in the fire" (Deuteronomy 18:10). But because God is a God of mercy, His forgiveness and healing are available to anyone who seeks it, including those who choose to have an abortion.

Many who have experienced post-abortion healing and restoration have gone on to birth children and become powerful advocates for life.

If you have harshly judged someone for having an abortion, try to appreciate the pain that person will feel when she realizes the significance of her decision. A woman in this situation needs our compassion, understanding and prayers, not our rejection. It is important to offer her forgiveness and moral support while also encouraging her to forgive herself and others who may have pressured her into seeking an abortion.

Scriptures on Forgiveness

Have mercy on me, O God, according to your unfailing love; according to your great compassion blot out my transgressions. Wash away all my iniquity and cleanse me from my sin. For I know my transgressions, and my sin is always before me. Against you, you only, have I sinned and done what is evil in your sight. . . . Cleanse me with hyssop, and I will be clean; wash me, and I will be whiter than snow. Let me hear joy and gladness; let the bones you have crushed rejoice. Hide your face from my sins and blot out all my iniquity (Psalm 51:1-4; 7-9).

Praise the LORD, O my soul, and forget not all his benefits— who forgives all your sins and heals all your diseases, who redeems your life from the pit and crowns you with love and compassion, who satisfies your desires with good things so that your youth is renewed like the eagle's. . . . As far as the east is from the west, so far has he removed our transgressions from us (Psalm 103:2-5,12).

I have swept away your offenses like a cloud, your sins like the morning mist. Return to me, for I have redeemed you (Isaiah 44:22).

If we confess our sins to him, he can be depended on to forgive us and to cleanse us from every wrong. [And it is perfectly proper for God to do this for us because Christ died to wash away our sins] (1 John 1:9, *TLB*).

Prayer Concerning Abortion

God, I come before You to confess my sin of destroying a life through abortion and to ask for Your mercy. Father, forgive me for my selfish act. Bring me into right relationship with You, and heal my painful memories and regret for making this choice. Thank You for Your promise that if we confess our sins, You are faithful and just to forgive us and to purify us. Lord, I receive Your forgiveness and cleansing and pray that You will strengthen me to walk in Your ways for the rest of my life, amen.

VICTORIOUS AND SINGLE

While God longs to give us a fulfilling life, Satan wants just the opposite. Some singles believe they will only be complete and useful to the Lord if and when they find a husband or wife. Not so! Don't accept that lie of the enemy. Single adults—whether widowed, divorced or never-married—are whole persons in themselves whom God can use in many ways to build His kingdom.

Singleness is not an obstacle to living a victorious life in the Lord, nor is it a problem to be solved. Some of Satan's tactics against godly singles include the following:

- Harassing them with chronic discontent so that they are unable to serve God joyfully while single
- Attacking their chastity by luring them into unholy and unhealthy alliances
- Trying to keep them from maintaining a pure and close relationship with the Lord
- Convincing them to believe the lie that without marriage they will remain incomplete and unfulfilled

The apostle Paul had the following word for singles in relationship to their opportunity to serve the Lord:

I would like you to be free from concern. An unmarried man is concerned about the Lord's affairs—how he can please the Lord. But a married man is concerned about the affairs of this world—how he can please his wife—and his interests are divided. An unmarried woman or virgin is concerned about the Lord's affairs: Her aim is to be devoted to the Lord in both

body and spirit. But a married woman is concerned about the
affairs of this world—how she can please her husband. I am
saying this for your own good, not to restrict you, but that
you may live in a right way in undivided devotion to the Lord
(1 Corinthians 7:32-35).

Paul does not say marriage is wrong. Rather, he advises a single person to give his or her "undivided devotion" to the Lord—meaning total
commitment and concentration on spiritual matters. To please the
Lord in every way—to be less concerned about the affairs of the world—
is both a challenge and opportunity to the unmarried Christian.
Michael Cavanaugh, who founded Mobilized to Serve, an international
ministry to single adults, has written in *God's Call to the Single Adult*:

Your singleness is a gift from God for service. As in no other
time in your life, your season as a single person sets you free
to serve God in a wholehearted and undistracted way. Unen-
cumbered by many of the duties and responsibilities that go
along with the married life, you are able to say "yes" to God in
a dynamic way. You are free to throw yourself with abandon
into the things of God—to know Him as you have never
known Him before, to love Him in an intimate way, and to
serve Him with all your heart, soul, mind and strength—one
hundred percent.[1]

Speaking to the student body at Christ for the Nations Institute,
Cavanaugh shared some of the following truths:

1. In Christ you have been made complete (see Colossians
   2:10). Jesus came to give you a full life right now. No human can give you worth or value except Jesus. To prepare
   for marriage, become the mightiest single person you can
   be for Jesus!

2. Recognize that marriage is not God's ultimate will for
   your life; it is to be conformed to the likeness of His son,
   Jesus (see Romans 8:29).

3. Your present singleness is the result of your choices. You could have married someone without standards. But you have chosen a certain standard—to follow Jesus.

4. Singleness is a gift from God for service, whether temporary or permanent. It's a gift of grace to walk victoriously in this season of your life while He is building His character in you.[2]

Jesus, in discussing marriage with His disciples, reminded them that in the beginning the Creator made man and woman with the intention that they form a monogamous family unit (see Matthew 19:5-6), but then He added, "Others have renounced marriage because of the kingdom of heaven" (Matthew 19:12). In other words, some men and women will remain single for life. Perhaps such a commitment will enable them to undertake a particular service for the Lord with greater freedom. Be attentive to the Lord and how He wants to guide your life.

God may direct you to relinquish certain relationships because He knows in the end they will not be beneficial and may, in fact, be damaging to you. The Holy Spirit gives comfort, strength and wisdom to those who obey this call. You can absolutely trust your future to the One who has your best interests at heart.

If you feel God does desire you to be married, it is still important to give wholehearted devotion to the Lord during the waiting period. Go where He wants you to go. Do what He wants you to do. Live life to the fullest, without thinking marriage is the answer to all your problems.

Waiting on God—Resisting the Enemy

Suppose God has planted a desire in your heart for a spouse. How can you combat temptation or impure thoughts while single? The answer sounds simple but requires discipline: Every time the enemy tries to make you feel sorry for yourself or urges you to indulge in sex outside of marriage, take authority over the enemy by audibly repeating the Word of God.

Maybe you feel you are in a waiting stage before your spouse comes along. What do you do? Pray. Wait for God's timing and be content in Him. Don't panic. Total commitment means trusting the Lord's plan and timing for your life. Whether you are single or married, fulfilling God's purpose for your life is of paramount importance.

Since God initiated family life, His archenemy, Satan, strives to disrupt godly marriages and to sabotage relationships between righteous people. Some pastors believe that Satan not only wants to kill babies through abortion but also wants to keep godly men and women from meeting, marrying and producing godly offspring.

Dr. Archibald Hart, a Christian psychologist, talks about men whose parents divorced and are now themselves often hesitant about marriage. However, his comments easily apply to others unwilling to make commitments:

> "Don't make commitments" is a life motto for many male adult children of divorce. This means that commitments of a personal nature should be avoided, so many of these men make heroic efforts to avoid being "tied down." This effort may involve many aspects of life—such as renting instead of buying or moving from job to job. But by far the most common result of this life-script is avoidance of commitment to relationships. These men typically put off marriage as long as possible—or avoid it altogether. The decision to live together without marriage is often a consequence of this life-script. So are quick divorces. The sheer disposability of marriage breeds a faulty attitude toward commitment. . . . If you never commit yourself to anyone, you never get hurt.[3]

Scriptures

Find rest, O my soul, in God alone; my hope comes from him (Psalm 62:5).

The LORD will fulfill [his purpose] for me; your love, O LORD, endures forever—do not abandon the works of your hands (Psalm 138:8).

Trust in the LORD with all your heart and lean not on your own understanding; in all your ways acknowledge him, and he will make your paths straight (Proverbs 3:5-6).

Commit to the LORD whatever you do, and your plans will succeed (Proverbs 16:3).

Many are the plans in a man's heart, but it is the LORD'S purpose that prevails (Proverbs 19:21).

Sing, O Daughter of Zion; shout aloud, O Israel! Be glad and rejoice with all your heart, O Daughter of Jerusalem! The LORD your God is with you, he is mighty to save. He will take great delight in you, he will quiet you with his love, he will rejoice over you with singing (Zephaniah 3:14,17).

He who unites himself with the Lord is one with him in spirit. Flee from sexual immorality. . . . Do you not know that your body is a temple of the Holy Spirit, who is in you, whom you have received from God? You are not your own; you were bought at a price. Therefore honor God with your body (1 Corinthians 6:17-20).

Always pray with joy . . . being confident of this, that he who began a good work in you will carry it on to completion until the day of Christ Jesus (Philippians 1:4-6).

I have learned the secret of being content in any and every situation, whether well fed or hungry, whether living in plenty or in want. I can do everything through him who gives me strength (Philippians 4:12-13).

Godliness with contentment is great gain (1 Timothy 6:6).

Flee the evil desires of youth, and pursue righteousness, faith, love and peace, along with those who call on the Lord out of a pure heart (2 Timothy 2:22).

Prayer

Lord, thank You that I am complete in You and that You are conforming me to Your image. I pray that Your mercy and grace will enable me to keep myself pure and to be content where You have placed me. My desire is to please You more than anyone; help me to do that, Lord. If there are relationships in my life I should end, please show them to me clearly and give me strength to obey You. Help me to walk in victory, with my life exhibiting the fruit of the Holy Spirit, as I trust You to direct my future. Amen.

MATERIAL PROVISION

Job layoffs . . . bankruptcies . . . buy-outs . . . plant closings . . . shortages of affordable housing . . . rising mortgage rates . . . soaring living costs. The trigger of economic pressures can ignite marital strife, alienation in families, addictions, anger and even riots. Are Christians immune to these realities that permeate our society? Not at all.

Financial difficulties can easily strike fear into the heart of anyone who loses sight of God's promises to provide for us. Normally self-sufficient believers can suddenly feel like a rudderless boat bobbing on a choppy sea of uncertainty, fearing they will shipwreck on the rocks of despair.

Should we blame the devil for such a crisis? Is it our own fault? Where is God in all this? Our culture fosters the notion that the answer is to find the culprit for our troubles and put the blame there—maybe even file a lawsuit. The "blame game" began with Adam, who blamed Eve for offering him forbidden fruit. She in turn blamed the serpent for deceiving her (see Genesis 3:11-13).

Ever since, we've been blaming one another or the government or the devil for the difficulties we suffer. Jesus identified the one most responsible when He said: "The thief [Satan] comes only to steal and kill and destroy; I have come that they may have life, and have it to the full" (John 10:10).

Although our own poor choices may contribute to the problem, the devil's strategies lurk behind the calamities that rob us of financial security. He is the source of all evil. When hard times hit close to home, he uses each problem as an opportunity to malign God and His faithfulness, to kill our hope and destroy our faith. In the midst of distress, Satan wants us to blame God rather than call on Him and acknowledge Him as our source of help.

We have a choice: either buy into the temptation to blame God and others, or take responsibility for our own actions and attitudes, seeking forgiveness for those that are wrong and trusting God in the areas where we have no control. We can choose to agree with Jesus' declaration: "I have come that they may have life, and have it to the full."

The word translated "life" here means "life in all its manifestations . . . life in activity . . . resurrection life and eternal life."[1] In other words, Jesus' purpose for coming to earth was to provide a way for us to live a meaningful life at every level and in every dimension—spiritual, physical and emotional.

Why We Suffer Need

God created Adam and Eve, placed them in the Garden and made every provision for their care. They had no need to worry about anything! But when these forebears of ours chose to disobey God's command, they brought a curse upon themselves and upon all humankind. "By the sweat of your brow you will eat your food," God declared (Genesis 3:19). When He thrust them out of the Garden to fend for themselves, anxiety about the future became our legacy.

However, because of His great mercy, God made covenant promises to His people. In the first fourteen verses of Deuteronomy 28, He spells out the blessings that will be given to those who diligently obey His commands. This is His promise in regard to provision: "The LORD will grant you abundant prosperity. . . . The LORD will open the heavens, the storehouse of his bounty, to send rain on your land in season and to bless all the work of your hands" (vv. 11a-12a). The keys to enjoying God's provision are:

1. Obey His Word, particularly in regard to tithing our income.

2. Keep our eyes and hearts focused on Him, not just on His blessings.

3. Resist the enemy's emphasis on how negative the circumstances may appear.

4. Be concerned about the needs of others and reach out to them.

Jesus taught this foundational principle to His disciples:

Therefore I tell you, do not worry about your life, what you will eat or drink; or about your body, what you will wear. Is not life more important than food, and the body more important than clothes? . . . For the pagans run after all these things, and your heavenly Father knows that you need them. But seek first his kingdom and his righteousness, and all these things will be given to you as well (Matthew 6:25,32-33).

Believers who abide by the principle of tithing feel that it is also a vital key to their having God's blessing of provision. The Scriptures say:

"Will a man rob God? Yet you rob me. "But you ask, 'How do we rob you?' "In tithes and offerings. You are under a curse—the whole nation of you—because you are robbing me. Bring the whole tithe into the storehouse, that there may be food in my house. Test me in this," says the LORD Almighty, "and see if I will not throw open the floodgates of heaven and pour out so much blessing that you will not have room enough for it. I will prevent pests from devouring your crops, and the vines in your fields will not cast their fruit," says the LORD Almighty (Malachi 3:8-11).

Dr. Harold Lindsell says of this passage:

Malachi insists that failure to tithe is to rob God of what rightfully belongs to him. And as a result, the divine blessing is withheld from those who refuse to give God his due. Tithing is not commanded in the New Testament as a legal requirement, but the Christian under grace can hardly do less than the Jew under law. Tithing is the outward sign of an inward commitment that all one has belongs to God, who is entitled to a return on the divine investment in any individual.[2]

Believers who meet the requirement of obedience can still claim God's promises of blessing and provision today. But obedience also entails showing concern and generosity toward others. God punished the disobedience of Ananias and Sapphira by death, as recorded in Acts 5:1-11. Contrast God's swift judgment of greed and selfishness with Paul's message: "For even when I was in Thessalonica, you sent me aid again and again when I was in need. . . . And my God will meet all your needs according to his glorious riches in Christ Jesus" (Philippians 4:16,19).

If you are faithful in tithing and giving, you can "rebuke the devourer" (Malachi 3:11, *KJV*) by reminding him of God's abundant promise of provision in the Scriptures.

Scriptures

If you follow my decrees and are careful to obey my commands, I will send you rain in its season, and the ground will yield its crops and the trees of the field their fruit. Your threshing will continue until grape harvest and the grape harvest will continue until planting, and you will eat all the food you want and live in safety in your land. . . . You will still be eating last year's harvest when you will have to move it out to make room for the new (Leviticus 26:3-5,10).

A tithe of everything from the land, whether grain from the soil or fruit from the trees, belongs to the LORD; it is holy to the LORD (Leviticus 27:30).

When you have eaten and are satisfied, praise the LORD your God for the good land he has given you. Be careful that you do not forget the LORD your God, failing to observe his commands, his laws and his decrees. . . . For it is he who gives you the ability to produce wealth, and so confirms his covenant, which he swore to your forefathers (Deuteronomy 8:10-11,18).

The LORD is my shepherd, I shall not be in want. He makes me lie down in green pastures, he leads me beside quiet waters, he restores my soul. He guides me in paths of righteousness for his name's sake. Even though I walk through the valley of the shadow of death, I will fear no evil, for you are with me;

your rod and your staff, they comfort me. You prepare a table before me in the presence of my enemies. You anoint my head with oil; my cup overflows. Surely goodness and love will follow me all the days of my life, and I will dwell in the house of the LORD forever (Psalm 23).

Great are the works of the LORD; they are pondered by all who delight in them. . . . He provides food for those who fear him; he remembers his covenant forever (Psalm 111:2,5).

Honor the LORD with your wealth, with the firstfruits of all your crops; then your barns will be filled to overflowing, and your vats will brim over with new wine (Proverbs 3:9-10).

If you spend yourselves in behalf of the hungry and satisfy the needs of the oppressed, then your light will rise in the darkness, and your night will become like the noonday. The LORD will guide you always; he will satisfy your needs in a sun-scorched land and will strengthen your frame. You will be like a well-watered garden, like a spring whose waters never fail (Isaiah 58:10-11).

Give, and it will be given to you. A good measure, pressed down, shaken together and running over, will be poured into your lap. For with the measure you use, it will be measured to you (Luke 6:38).

He who did not spare his own Son, but gave him up for us all—how will he not also, along with him, graciously give us all things? (Romans 8:32).

For you know the grace of our Lord Jesus Christ, that though he was rich, yet for your sakes he became poor, so that you through his poverty might become rich (2 Corinthians 8:9).

Remember this: Whoever sows sparingly will also reap sparingly, and whoever sows generously will also reap generously.

Each man should give what he has decided in his heart to give, not reluctantly or under compulsion, for God loves a cheerful giver. And God is able to make all grace abound to you, so that in all things at all times, having all that you need, you will abound in every good work (2 Corinthians 9:6-8).

Now he who supplies seed to the sower and bread for food will also supply and increase your store of seed and will enlarge the harvest of your righteousness. You will be made rich in every way so that you can be generous on every occasion, and through us your generosity will result in thanksgiving to God (2 Corinthians 9:10-11).

Command those who are rich in this present world not to be arrogant nor to put their hope in wealth, which is so uncertain, but to put their hope in God, who richly provides us with everything for our enjoyment. Command them to do good, to be rich in good deeds, and to be generous and willing to share. In this way they will lay up treasure for themselves as a firm foundation for the coming age, so that they may take hold of the life that is truly life (1 Timothy 6:17-19).

Cast all your anxiety on him because he cares for you (1 Peter 5:7).

Prayer

Thank You, Father, that as I am faithful to tithe in obedience to Your Word, I can claim Your promises to provide for my needs. I acknowledge You as the source of everything I need for my spirit, soul and body. Lord, help me to be generous in reaching out to the needs of others, even as I trust You for my own. I choose to cast all my care and anxiety upon You, knowing that You care for me, Your child. I praise You for Your faithfulness, in Jesus' name, amen.

PROTECTION AND SECURITY

"God is our refuge and strength, an ever-present help in trouble" (Psalm 46:1). When disaster—or even the fear of trouble—looms larger than life on our horizon, we need assurance of God's protection. In searching the Word of God, we find many reminders of His promises of protection that give us a sense of security.

One helpful approach is to find in Scripture the story of someone's dilemma comparable to the one confronting you, and then discover how the matter was resolved with God's help. Ask the Holy Spirit to guide your study. In the process, you often can find verses to use as ammunition in your spiritual warfare as well as to keep yourself encouraged. Psalm 91, for example, offers dramatic assurance that the Lord will protect and rescue His child:

> He who dwells in the shelter of the Most High will rest in the shadow of the Almighty. I will say of the LORD, "He is my refuge and my fortress, my God, in whom I trust."
>
> Surely he will save you from the fowler's snare and from the deadly pestilence. He will cover you with his feathers, and under his wings you will find refuge; his faithfulness will be your shield and rampart. You will not fear the terror of night, nor the arrow that flies by day, nor the pestilence that stalks in the darkness, nor the plague that destroys at midday. A thousand may fall at your side, ten thousand at your right hand, but it will not come near you. You will only observe with your eyes and see the punishment of the wicked.
>
> If you make the Most High your dwelling—even the LORD, who is my refuge—then no harm will befall you, no disaster will come near your tent. For he will command his angels concerning you to guard you in all your ways; they will lift you up in their hands, so that you will not strike your foot against

a stone. You will tread upon the lion and the cobra; you will trample the great lion and the serpent.

"Because he loves me," says the LORD, "I will rescue him; I will protect him, for he acknowledges my name. He will call upon me, and I will answer him; I will be with him in trouble, I will deliver him and honor him. With long life will I satisfy him and show him my salvation."

Remove Desecration

Notice that the promise of Psalm 91 has a condition attached: We must make the Most High our dwelling-place if we want His protection. One way of doing so is to honor Him by dedicating our home to Him, inviting His presence to abide in our home, and seeing to it that we not allow any detestable things to remain there (see Deuteronomy 7:25-26). The same principle applies to our offices, hotel rooms, vacation cottages—anywhere and everywhere we spend time. Thomas White explains:

> Evil spirits can pollute places with their unholy presence. Such demonization usually occurs when mortal beings commit immoral acts that open the door to the activity of demons. For example, a house used for the manufacture or selling of drugs, a place used for prostitution, or a building used by a fortune-teller or spiritualist group may invite demons of bondage, deception, violence, lust, sexual perversion, or familiar spirits of the occult. Even when the perpetrators have left the scene, evil spirits may linger, hoping to prey upon unsuspecting newcomers.[1]

It is important to rid your dwelling of any object that even hints of occult involvement or idol worship. Some Christians returning from trips abroad innocently bring back artifacts such as fetishes, face masks, "sacred" writings or carved figures of false gods, among other things, which may have been used in idol worship in some way. God gave clear instructions in these matters:

> The images of their gods you are to burn in the fire. Do not covet the silver and gold on them, and do not take it for yourselves, or you will be ensnared by it, for it is detestable to the

LORD your God. Do not bring a detestable thing into your house. . . . Utterly abhor and detest it, for it is set apart for destruction (Deuteronomy 7:25-26).

Josiah, one of Judah's kings, offers a biblical example of obedience in the matter: "Furthermore, Josiah got rid of the mediums and spiritists, the household gods, the idols and all the other detestable things seen in Judah and Jerusalem. This he did to fulfill the requirements of the law written in the book that Hilkiah the priest had discovered in the temple of the LORD" (2 Kings 23:24).

When Paul evangelized in Ephesus, the new converts wasted no time in cleaning house: "A number who had practiced sorcery brought their scrolls together and burned them publicly. When they calculated the value of the scrolls, the total came to fifty thousand drachmas" (Acts 19:19).

The following Scriptures can prove helpful as you build your faith in God's protection and security, no matter how vulnerable your present situation may seem. Remember to speak the Word aloud. Our proclamation of the truth is heard by a vast invisible world—God and His angels, as well as Satan and his demonic hosts. We invoke God's protection to shield us from enemy assaults. We strengthen our own faith as we hear ourselves affirm the truth of God.

Scriptures on God's Protection and Security

I will lie down and sleep in peace, for you alone, O LORD, make me dwell in safety (Psalm 4:8).

For in the day of trouble he will keep me safe in his dwelling; he will hide me in the shelter of his tabernacle and set me high upon a rock (Psalm 27:5).

The LORD is my strength and my shield; my heart trusts in him, and I am helped. My heart leaps for joy and I will give thanks to him in song (Psalm 28:7).

The LORD watches over you— the LORD is your shade at your right hand; the sun will not harm you by day, nor the moon by night. The LORD will keep you from all harm—he will watch over your life; the LORD will watch over your coming and going both now and forevermore (Psalm 121:5-8).

Keep me, O LORD, from the hands of the wicked; protect me from men of violence who plan to trip my feet. Proud men have hidden a snare for me; they have spread out the cords of their net and have set traps for me along my path. O LORD, I say to you, "You are my God." Hear, O LORD, my cry for mercy (Psalm 140:4-6).

Even to your old age and gray hairs I am he, I am he who will sustain you. I have made you and I will carry you; I will sustain you and I will rescue you (Isaiah 46:4).

The LORD is good, a refuge in times of trouble. He cares for those who trust in him (Nahum 1:7).

God is just: He will pay back trouble to those who trouble you and give relief to you who are troubled, and to us as well. This will happen when the Lord Jesus is revealed from heaven in blazing fire with his powerful angels (2 Thessalonians 1:6-7).

The Lord is faithful, and he will strengthen and protect you from the evil one (2 Thessalonians 3:3).

Scriptures on God as Our Shield

My God is my rock, in whom I take refuge, my shield and the horn of my salvation. He is my stronghold, my refuge and my savior—from violent men you save me (2 Samuel 22:3).

As for God, his way is perfect; the word of the LORD is flawless. He is a shield for all who take refuge in him (2 Samuel 22:31).

For surely, O LORD, you bless the righteous; you surround them with your favor as with a shield (Psalm 5:12).

You give me your shield of victory, and your right hand sustains me; you stoop down to make me great (Psalm 18:35).

You are my refuge and my shield; I have put my hope in your word (Psalm 119:114).

Praise be to the LORD my Rock, who trains my hands for war, my fingers for battle. He is my loving God and my fortress, my stronghold and my deliverer, my shield, in whom I take refuge, who subdues peoples under me (Psalm 144:1-2).

Prayer

Lord, may I always dwell in Your shelter, for You are my refuge and my fortress. You are my God. I trust You to answer me when I am in trouble and to deliver me. Thank You that You are a shield round about me. Whenever I am afraid, I will declare that You are there, watching over me with protection and security. I give You praise for Your faithfulness, in Jesus' name, amen.

PART IV

STANDING IN THE GAP

HEALING

Sickness, along with sin and separation from God, is a painful result of man's rebellion against God. That first sin in the Garden destroyed human innocence and opened a veritable floodgate, allowing rivers of sin to wash over the human race. Sickness, pain and death also came crashing through that gate.

We inherit from Adam and Eve both our inclination to sin and our vulnerability to sickness and disease. However, God's solution was to send His Son as the perfect sacrifice, not only to atone for our sin, but also to provide healing of soul, mind and body. Speaking of Jesus, Isaiah prophesied:

> Surely he took up our infirmities and carried our sorrows, yet we considered him stricken by God, smitten by him, and afflicted. But he was pierced for our transgressions, he was crushed for our iniquities; the punishment that brought us peace was upon him, and by his wounds we are healed (Isaiah 53:4-5).

Divine health is God's best for us. Yet many factors—some our own fault, some because we are members of a fallen race, some the work of the enemy—frustrate God's plan. His higher plan, however, is to conform us to the image of His Son (see Romans 8:29).

Healing clearly was important to Jesus. He not only healed the sick Himself, but He also commissioned His followers to do the same:

> He called his twelve disciples to him and gave them authority to drive out evil spirits and to heal every disease and sickness. . . . These twelve Jesus sent out with the following instructions: "Heal the sick, raise the dead, cleanse those who

have leprosy, drive out demons. Freely you have received, freely give" (Matthew 10:1,5,8).

God's power to heal has not diminished one bit today. And He continues to search for disciples who will pray for the sick. God touches sick bodies with His healing power every day. Sometimes our prayer and spiritual warfare is coupled with modern medical technology. Other times we may see instant miracles. In some cases, prayer can help to accelerate the body's efforts to heal itself.

Our Privilege of Prayer

Our privilege is to pray for healing, and God's prerogative is to heal in His own way and timing. We cooperate with Him by reminding ourselves and the devil of God's promise of healing through the blood of Jesus Christ. But it's important to guard against insisting on our own "formula" of exactly how and when God will heal.

We may see that our prayers for healing prolong a person's life, yet we don't see the total healing for which we had hoped. Such an outcome does not necessarily mean defeat. We must recognize that prayer and spiritual warfare can extend life to allow people time to "get their house in order"—both in spiritual and in practical matters—or time to accomplish a particular task or goal in life that God intends them to do.

As spiritual warriors, we should focus our attention on Jesus—to worship, love and know Him in an intimate way, even in the midst of pain and distress. Ask for wisdom and discernment as to how to pray for a needed healing, and then engage in prayer and spiritual warfare and trust the Lord to intervene in miraculous ways.

The Important Factor of Obedience

It is unreasonable to habitually disobey God's natural and spiritual laws and yet expect Him to keep us well. Recognizing that our body is the temple of the Holy Spirit, we should use good sense in not abusing it with harmful substances or foods that lack nutrition, or in failing to get proper rest. Failure to properly care for our bodies increases the likelihood that sickness will result.

In some cases, unforgiveness may be at the root of an illness. It's essential to forgive anyone against whom you hold a grudge or complaint and confess any known sin. Ask God to show you if such issues need to be dealt with and then, if such issues do exist, repent, ask Him to forgive you, and receive and accept His forgiveness.

Of course, we must not assume that just because someone has a sickness, they have necessarily sinned—or that they lack faith to believe God for healing. We should pray—and encourage the one suffering to pray—for an understanding of the cause of the illness and for direction on the course of action to follow.

Dean Sherman reminds us that sickness can have reasons other than being caused by the devil:

> Sickness can be caused by germs. Most often we are sick, not because of the devil, nor because of sin in our lives, nor because of the judgment from God. We are sick from bacteria, viruses, or physiological abnormalities. This is the world in which we live. We may be sick because of inherent weaknesses. . . . Sickness can also be the result of abuse to our bodies. Improper diet, lack of exercise, or lack of rest may bring illness.[1]

In our book *Lord, I Need Your Healing Power: Securing God's Help in Sickness and Trials*, we point out that many of us may need to modify how and what we eat, remembering that our bodies are temples of the Holy Spirit (see 1 Corinthians 6:19). Temptations abound: fried fast foods, sugar-loaded drinks, oversize portions, a vast array of fattening snacks and a sedentary lifestyle. Jesus' teaching was of health, wholeness and salvation.[2]

Sample Scripture Warfare

Before praying for healing, you (and/or the person you are praying for) must forgive anyone against whom you hold a grudge or grievance and confess any known sin. Ask God to forgive you; then receive and accept His forgiveness. You may want to make declarations based on Bible verses something like this adaptation of Colossians 2:13-15:

> God has made me alive with Christ. He forgave all my sins, having canceled the written code [doctor's reports, negative

words, and so forth] that stood opposed to me and, having taken it away, nailed it to the cross. And having disarmed the powers and authorities, He made a public spectacle of them, triumphing over them by the cross.

A mother we know used this Scripture when praying for her child who was mentally challenged. Despite his poor grades and several negative reports from his teachers, she "canceled" these reports by praying a paraphrased version of these verses. Her son began to improve and was able to graduate from high school.[3]

The Word of God is the basis of our faith for healing; thus, immersing yourself in Scripture and declaring it aloud will strengthen your faith to trust God for His intervention (see Romans 10:17). The following is a sampling of verses on healing from God's Word.

Healing Scriptures

O LORD my God, I called to you for help and you healed me. O LORD, you brought me up from the grave; you spared me from going down into the pit. Sing to the LORD, you saints of his; praise his holy name (Psalm 30:2-3).

Forget not all his benefits—who forgives all your sins and heals all your diseases, who redeems your life from the pit and crowns you with love and compassion (Psalm 103:2-4).

They cried to the LORD in their trouble, and he saved them from their distress. He sent forth his word and healed them; he rescued them from the grave (Psalm 107:19-20).

My son, pay attention to what I say; listen closely to my words. Do not let them out of your sight, keep them within your heart; for they are life to those who find them and health to a man's whole body (Proverbs 4:20-21).

A cheerful heart is good medicine, but a crushed spirit dries up the bones (Proverbs 17:22).

Heal me, O LORD, and I will be healed; save me and I will be saved, for you are the one I praise (Jeremiah 17:14).

Jesus went throughout Galilee, teaching in their synagogues, preaching the good news of the kingdom, and healing every disease and sickness among the people (Matthew 4:23).

Just then a woman who had been subject to bleeding for twelve years came up behind him [Jesus] and touched the edge of his cloak. She said to herself, "If I only touch his cloak, I will be healed." Jesus turned and saw her. "Take heart, daughter," he said, "your faith has healed you." And the woman was healed from that moment (Matthew 9:20-22).

When he had gone indoors, the blind men came to him, and he asked them, "Do you believe that I am able to do this?" "Yes, Lord," they replied. Then he touched their eyes and said, "According to your faith will it be done to you"; and their sight was restored (Matthew 9:28-29).

Great crowds came to him [Jesus], bringing the lame, the blind, the crippled, the mute and many others, and laid them at his feet; and he healed them. The people were amazed when they saw the mute speaking, the crippled made well, the lame walking and the blind seeing. And they praised the God of Israel (Matthew 15:30-31).

And these signs will accompany those who believe: In my name [the name of Jesus] they will drive out demons; . . . they will place their hands on sick people, and they will get well (Mark 16:17-18).

He [Jesus] welcomed them and spoke to them about the kingdom of God, and healed those who needed healing (Luke 9:11).

The apostles performed many miraculous signs and wonders among the people. . . . More and more men and women

believed in the Lord and were added to their number. As a result, people brought the sick into the streets and laid them on
beds and mats so that at least Peter's shadow might fall on some
of them as he passed by. Crowds gathered also from the towns
around Jerusalem, bringing their sick and those tormented by
evil spirits, and all of them were healed (Acts 5:12-16).

In Lystra there sat a man crippled in his feet, who was lame
from birth and had never walked. He listened to Paul as he was
speaking. Paul looked directly at him, saw that he had faith to
be healed and called out, "Stand up on your feet!" At that, the
man jumped up and began to walk (Acts 14:8-10).

God did extraordinary miracles through Paul, so that even
handkerchiefs and aprons that had touched him were taken to
the sick, and their illnesses were cured and the evil spirits left
them (Acts 19:11-12).

Is any one of you sick? He should call the elders of the church
to pray over him and anoint him with oil in the name of the
Lord. And the prayer offered in faith will make the sick person
well; the Lord will raise him up. If he has sinned, he will be forgiven. Therefore confess your sins to each other and pray for
each other so that you may be healed. The prayer of a righteous
man is powerful and effective (James 5:14-16).

He himself bore our sins in his body on the tree, so that we
might die to sins and live for righteousness; by his wounds you
have been healed (1 Peter 2:24).

Dear friend, I pray that you may enjoy good health and that all
may go well with you, even as your soul is getting along well
(3 John 2).

Prayer

*In the name of Jesus Christ, by the authority of His shed blood, we come
against every plot of Satan against [person's name]'s body. We thank*

You, Lord, that Your Word energizes and gives life and that You
are giving that life to [name] as we pray.

Father, bring healing and wholeness to the tissue, joints, marrow and
fiber, to the blood system and to the other systems of the body affected
by this illness. May the medications he/she is taking have a beneficial
effect, and all negative side effects be cancelled in Jesus' name.
Lord, cause his/her body to function as You created it to function.

We declare that the enemy's plan of destruction is null and void
because Christ defeated him at the cross. We cover [name] with the
blood of Jesus and ask You to strengthen him/her with might in the
inner man. We call upon the life that is in Jesus Christ to cause the
enemy to flee. We thank You for victory, in Jesus' name. Amen.

DELIVERANCE

Ever since the archangel Lucifer and his cohorts were cast out of heaven, they have been opposing God's kingdom and His plan for mankind to take dominion in the earth. Lucifer, renamed Satan, began his destructive work in the Garden when he deceived Adam and Eve. His continued strategies against the human race have been relentless, as we've seen in our own lives, in the lives of our loved ones and in the nations of the world. E. M. Bounds states:

> Satan sows the tares in the wheat . . . bad thoughts among good thoughts. All kinds of evil seed are sown by him in the harvest fields of earth. He is always trying to make the good bad and the bad worse. He fills the mind of Judas, and he inflames and hurries him on to his infamous purpose. . . . The devil goes about as fierce, as resolute, and as strong as a lion, intent only to destroy.[1]

Breaking Bondages

The good news of the Gospel is that Christ came "to destroy the devil's work" (1 John 3:8). And He told His followers, "I have given you authority . . . to overcome all the power of the enemy" (Luke 10:19). The word "all" here signifies the totality, every level, of power.

So why do we still see believers struggling against various bondages? Because somewhere they have left a door open that allows the enemy access to their lives. Some primary causes are disobeying God's Word, greed, unforgiveness, immorality, occult involvement, substance abuse, rebelling against spiritual authority, and spiritual pride. In most cases the problem begins when a person listens to the enemy's voice and compromises what he or she knows to be the truth. Consider these scriptural warnings:

Why do you call me, "Lord, Lord," and do not do what I say? (Luke 6:46).

Then Peter said, "Ananias, how is it that Satan has so filled your heart that you have lied to the Holy Spirit?" (Acts 5:3).

If you forgive anyone, I also forgive him. And what I have for-given—if there was anything to forgive—I have forgiven in the sight of Christ for your sake, in order that Satan might not outwit us. For we are not unaware of his schemes (2 Corinthians 2:10-11).

"In your anger do not sin": Do not let the sun go down while you are still angry, and do not give the devil a foothold (Ephesians 4:26-27).

Many people fail to take such scriptural warnings seriously, thus opening themselves to Satan's dark kingdom when they disobey God's written commands. If the enemy has a foothold in your life, ask the Holy Spirit to reveal to you how he gained access. You may need to seek ministry and counsel from a minister or prayer partner as you deal with those specific areas.

Finding the Root of the Problem

In our book *Lord, Help Me Break this Habit: You Can Be Free from Doing the Things You Hate*, we share about a young woman who began to be-lieve a lie that she was fat and always would be. Her eating and purg-ing binges led to her developing a serious eating disorder. During counseling she realized she had believed a lie about how she viewed herself. "I had to take responsibility for my own choices and stop blaming my parents, my peers or anyone else for the disappointments in my life," she said.[2]

When she forgave herself, memorized Scripture and continued counseling, she experienced a wonderful breakthrough. Whenever the enemy again whispered to her, "You are fat," she would repeat her per-sonal adaptation of 1 Corinthians 10:13, a verse that became her life-line: "No temptation has seized me except what is common to man.

And God is faithful; He will not let me be tempted beyond what I can
bear. But when I am tempted, He will also provide a way out so that I
can stand up under it." She often prayed, "Lord, provide the way of
escape when I'm tempted to overeat." In the ensuing years she has kept
her weight down, stopped her hateful self-talk and found a reason-
able exercise routine. Today, she is a radiant woman.[3]

If you are counseling or praying for an individual who needs deliverance, ask the Holy Spirit for revelation concerning the root cause
of the problem. This is particularly important because if you deal only
with the symptom—the outward behavior—without getting to the root
of the matter, the problem will only recur.

Study biblical examples of the devil's tactics. Remember that Satan is only a fallen archangel; never see him as an equal to God. To
paint a clearer picture of the enemy's domain, Dean Sherman describes who inhabits the kingdom of darkness:

> Satan (an individual fallen archangel) and fallen angels, nu-
> merous demons, and evil spirits. According to God's Word,
> that is all there is. These spirits are personalities. . . . Jesus
> didn't confront a force of evil. He confronted evil spirits,
> sometimes naming them by name. . . . Like all personalities,
> fallen angels think, listen, communicate, experience, act, and
> react. They speak to us in our minds. . . . They hear what we
> say, watch our reactions, and make plans and strategies. Be-
> cause these evil personalities listen, we need to speak to them
> when we do spiritual warfare . . . rebuking them and verbally
> denying them access to our lives. Jesus addressed the enemy
> directly. Having told us that we would do greater things than
> he, Jesus has shown us by example that we too should address
> the enemy, resisting him.[4]

Binding the Enemy

As intercessors we stand between God and a person, asking God to
intervene for his or her need. But we also stand between Satan and
that person, battling and pushing back the powers of darkness.

To bind evil spirits means to restrain them by speaking directly
to them and forbidding them to continue their destructive activity.

The Holy Spirit's power energizes our words to release the person from the enemy's hold. Then in prayer we ask the Holy Spirit to minister to that person's need, to help him or her walk in obedience to God's Word. Also, we pray that the person will learn to exercise authority over the enemy according to 1 Peter 5:8-9.

Jesus Himself provides a model for dealing boldly and authoritatively with demonic powers: "If I drive out demons by the Spirit of God, then the kingdom of God has come upon you. . . . How can anyone enter a strong man's house and carry off his possessions unless he first ties up the strong man? Then he can rob his house" (Matthew 12:28-29).

Jesus also told His followers: "I will give you the keys of the kingdom of heaven; whatever you bind on earth will be bound in heaven, and whatever you loose on earth will be loosed in heaven" (Matthew 16:19).

Learning from Jesus' Ministry

Seven gospel stories illustrate our Lord's deliverance ministry:

1. the dumb demoniac (Matthew 9:32-34)
2. the blind/dumb demoniac (Matthew 12:22-24)
3. the synagogue demoniac (Mark 1:21-28; Luke 4:31-37)
4. the Gerasene demoniac(s) (Matthew 8:28-34; Mark 5:1-20; Luke 8:26-39)
5. the Syrophoenician woman's daughter (Matthew 15:21-28; Mark 7:24-30)
6. the epileptic boy (Matthew 17:14-20; Mark 9:14-29; Luke 9:37-43)
7. the woman bent with a spirit of infirmity (Luke 13:10-17)

News about him [Jesus] spread all over Syria, and people brought to him all who were ill with various diseases, those suffering severe pain, the demon-possessed, those having seizures, and the paralyzed, and he healed them (Matthew 4:24).

While they were going out, a man who was demon-possessed and could not talk was brought to Jesus. And when the demon was driven out, the man who had been mute spoke. The crowd was amazed and said, "Nothing like this has ever been seen in Israel" (Matthew 9:32-33).

Then they brought him a demon-possessed man who was blind and mute, and Jesus healed him, so that he could both talk and see. . . . When the Pharisees heard this, they said, "It is only by Beelzebub, the prince of demons, that this fellow drives out demons." Jesus knew their thoughts and said to them, ". . . If Satan drives out Satan, he is divided against himself. . . . But if I drive out demons by the Spirit of God, then the kingdom of God has come upon you" (Matthew 12:22-28).

A man in the crowd answered, "Teacher, I brought you my son, who is possessed by a spirit that has robbed him of speech. . . . I asked your disciples to drive out the spirit, but they could not." He [Jesus] rebuked the evil spirit. "You deaf and mute spirit," he said, "I command you, come out of him and never enter him again." The spirit shrieked, convulsed him violently and came out (Mark 9:17-18,25-26).

When Jesus had called the Twelve together, he gave them power and authority to drive out all demons and to cure diseases, and he sent them out to preach the kingdom of God and to heal the sick (Luke 9:1-2).

On a Sabbath Jesus was teaching in one of the synagogues, and a woman was there who had been crippled by a spirit for eighteen years. She was bent over and could not straighten up at all. When Jesus saw her, he called her forward and said to her, "Woman, you are set free from your infirmity." Then he put his hands on her, and immediately she straightened up and praised God. . . . The Lord answered him, "Should not this woman, a daughter of Abraham, whom Satan has kept bound for eighteen long years, be set free on the Sabbath day from what bound her?" (Luke 13:10-16).

God anointed Jesus of Nazareth with the Holy Spirit and power, and . . . he went around doing good and healing all who were under the power of the devil, because God was with him (Acts 10:38).

Doing What Jesus Did

During the days of Jesus' ministry on earth the apostles sometimes had difficulty freeing demonized people from Satan's bondage, as seen in the case of the epileptic boy whose father asked for their help. But before He went to the cross, Jesus declared, "Anyone who has faith in me will do what I have been doing. He will do even greater things than these, because I am going to the Father" (John 14:12). That promise was not strictly for the apostles; it is for "anyone who has faith." After they were filled with the Holy Spirit, the apostles walked in boldness and authority:

> Once when we were going to the place of prayer, we were met by a slave girl who had a spirit by which she predicted the future. She earned a great deal of money for her owners by fortune-telling. This girl followed Paul and the rest of us, shouting, "These men are servants of the Most High God, who are telling you the way to be saved." She kept this up for many days. Finally Paul became so troubled that he turned around and said to the spirit, "In the name of Jesus Christ I command you to come out of her!" At that moment the spirit left her (Acts 16:16-18).

> Dear friends, do not believe every spirit, but test the spirits to see whether they are from God, because many false prophets have gone out into the world. This is how you can recognize the Spirit of God: Every spirit that acknowledges that Jesus Christ has come in the flesh is from God, but every spirit that does not acknowledge Jesus is not from God. This is the spirit of the antichrist, which you have heard is coming and even now is already in the world (1 John 4:1-3).

Dr. Neil Anderson, in his book *The Bondage Breaker*, states that we need to see the issue of confronting the demonic as a truth encounter, not a power encounter. He writes:

The power for Christian living is found in the truth; the power of Satan is in the lie. Satan does not want you to know your power and authority as a believer in Christ because his power is only effective in the dark. . . . Satan fears detection more than anything else. Whenever the light of truth comes on, he and his demons, like cockroaches, head for the shadows. . . . I do everything I can to prevent Satan from manifesting himself and glorifying himself through a power encounter. We are to glorify *God* by allowing *His* presence to be manifested.[5]

Prayer

Father, just as Jesus prayed that You would protect His disciples from the evil one, we ask that You also protect us by the power of His name. Reveal to us any area of our lives where we have allowed the enemy access. Help us to repent and then walk in obedience to Your Word. Give us Your strategy to defeat the schemes and devices of the evil one. May we be fully armed and equipped to declare the truth and expose the devil's strategies against us and our loved ones.

Thank You for the Holy Spirit who empowers us. Thank You for Jesus' shed blood on the cross that bought our deliverance at so great a price. Thank You that we can overcome by the blood of the Lamb, the Word of God and our testimony. We rejoice in Your victory!
Amen.

INTERCESSION FOR OTHERS

"Without God, we cannot. Without us, God will not." St. Augustine's succinct statement sums up the twofold nature of intercession. God empowers us by the Holy Spirit to intercede for others' needs; without that empowerment our prayers would be empty words.

God also invests us with Christ's authority to restrain satanic forces that are blinding and hindering the person for whom we are praying. God could restrain those forces without us if He chose to. But he has equipped us and commissioned us to intercede by pushing back the enemy, thus allowing the Holy Spirit to bring conviction that leads to repentance.

Two Old Testament verses depict the need for an intercessor to do battle for sinful humankind: "He [God] was appalled that there was no one to intervene" (Isaiah 59:16); "I [God] looked for a man among them who would build up the wall and stand before me in the gap on behalf of the land so I would not have to destroy it, but I found none" (Ezekiel 22:30). Bible teacher Joy Dawson says these verses depict God's quest:

> The heart of God is searching for those who will answer the need for someone to stand in the gap. The picture is clear: Without someone in place, invasion of the darkness occurs, and eventual destruction of people takes place. Answer the Holy Spirit's call. Don't allow the price that needs to be paid make intercession a passive issue. It will cost time, energy, sleep, purity of motive, and greater faith than most other things we do. . . . God has made it clear from Genesis to Revelation that prayer is the match that lights the fuse to release the explosive power of the Holy Spirit in the affairs of men. Let us give it priority time.[1]

Of course, Jesus ultimately filled that gap. He became the mediator between God and man by giving Himself as a sacrifice for sin. But believers are also called to be intercessors.

Following a Biblical Model for Intercession

Joshua's battle with the Amalekites is a vivid example of the power of intercession. While Joshua and Israel's army fought, Moses, Aaron, and Hur interceded. God gave them victory, but it required the cooperation of the intercessors and an army of fighters:

> So Joshua fought the Amalekites as Moses had ordered, and Moses, Aaron and Hur went to the top of the hill. As long as Moses held up his hands, the Israelites were winning, but whenever he lowered his hands, the Amalekites were winning. When Moses' hands grew tired, they took a stone and put it under him and he sat on it. Aaron and Hur held his hands up—one on one side, one on the other—so that his hands remained steady till sunset. So Joshua overcame the Amalekite army with the sword (Exodus 17:10-13).

The Hebrew root word for intercessor or intercession is *paga* (paw-GAH), meaning "to come between, to assail, to cause to entreat."[2] When an Israeli soldier hits the mark in target practice, he shouts "*Paga!*"— the modern Hebrew equivalent of "Bull's eye!" Effective intercessors learn to hit the bull's eye with accuracy in their warfare.

Preparing for Intercession

Doubt, disobedience and unbelief cloud our spiritual vision, bring condemnation and prevent us from praying with faith and boldness. Just as the priests would cleanse themselves before going into God's presence to represent the people, so we need to prepare ourselves for the ministry of intercession. Repentance and a renewed commitment to obey the Lord make us ready to "approach the throne of grace with confidence" (Hebrews 4:16) and to take an offensive stand against the enemy.

Both the psalmist David and the apostle John emphasize this principle: "Create in me a pure heart, O God, and renew a steadfast spirit within me" (Psalm 51:10); "Dear friends, if our hearts do not condemn us, we have confidence before God and receive from him anything we ask, because we obey his commands and do what pleases him" (1 John 3:21-22).

Standing in the Gap

Why is it that some people seem apparently closed to the Gospel message? Are they indifferent to Jesus' sacrifice for their sins? The Bible offers some clues:

1. The god of this age has blinded the minds of unbelievers, so that they cannot see the light of the gospel of the glory of Christ (2 Corinthians 4:4).

2. Those who oppose him [the Lord's servant] he must gently instruct, in the hope that . . . they will come to their senses and escape from the trap of the devil, who has taken them captive to do his will (2 Timothy 2:25-26).

3. The worries of this life, the deceitfulness of wealth and the desires for other things come in and choke the word, making it unfruitful (Mark 4:19).

4. Ask the Lord of the harvest, therefore, to send out workers into his harvest field (Matthew 9:38).

God's Word tells us what kind of prayers to pray, who to pray for and why:

I urge, then, first of all, that requests, prayers, intercession and thanksgiving be made for everyone—for kings and all those in authority, that we may live peaceful and quiet lives in all godliness and holiness. This is good, and pleases God our Savior, who wants all men to be saved and to come to a knowledge of the truth (1 Timothy 2:1-4).

For this reason Christ is the mediator of a new covenant, that those who are called may receive the promised eternal inheritance—now that he has died as a ransom to set them free from the sins committed under the first covenant (Hebrews 9:15).

When the prophet Jeremiah was shut up in prison, the Lord wanted to reveal to him things in the future. He instructed Jeremiah, "Call to me and I will answer you and tell you great and unsearchable things you do not know" (Jeremiah 33:3). "Call" here means cry out—in an attempt to get one's attention—or proclaim. Dick Eastman explains this passage more thoroughly:

> God promised Jeremiah that if he would call to Him, not only would He answer him, but He would reveal to him "great and mighty" things that could not otherwise be known. The word "mighty" is better rendered "isolated" or "inaccessible." The suggestion is that God would give Jeremiah "revelational insight," revealing things that otherwise would be inaccessible or isolated. Such "revelational insight" always has been essential for a clear understanding of victorious spiritual warfare. One cannot pray effectively without insight into how to pray, as well as into what things God truly longs for us to seek after in prayer.[3]

Wrestling in Prayer

Paul was continually reminding believers in the Early Church to remain faithful in prayer. In one of his letters he mentions a coworker who was a faithful and hard-working intercessor: "Epaphras, who is one of you and a servant of Christ Jesus, sends greetings. He is always wrestling in prayer for you, that you may stand firm in all the will of God, mature and fully assured. I vouch for him that he is working hard for you and for those at Laodicea and Hierapolis" (Colossians 4:12-13).

The enemy uses whatever devices he can to keep those for whom we pray from coming to the knowledge of truth and receiving Jesus as Lord. To see them delivered may literally require that we wrestle in prayer as Epaphras did. But we're not alone in this important task. The Father provides a helper—the Holy Spirit—to help us hit the target in our prayers.

Dutch Sheets, in his book *Intercessory Prayer: How God Can Use Your Prayers to Move Heaven and Earth*, tells about watching as a building nearly the size of a city block was demolished by dynamite in less than 10 seconds. He likens this scene to intercession:

I like to think that this in some ways can also be a picture of our intercession. Unlike this physical building, we don't usually see the answer in seconds—we may be strategically placing the dynamite of the Spirit for days, weeks or months. But every time we take up our spiritual weapons and use them against the strongholds of the enemy, we are placing our explosive charges in strategic places. And sooner or later the Holy Detonator of Heaven is going to say, "Enough!" There will be a mighty explosion in the spirit, a stronghold will crumble to the ground and a person will fall to their knees. [4]

Sheets believes that Scriptures indicate our prayers accumulate:

There are bowls in heaven in which our prayers are stored . . . I don't know if it's literal or symbolic. It doesn't matter. The principle is still the same. God has something in which He stores our prayers for use at the proper time.

"And when He had taken the book, the four living creatures and the twenty-four elders fell down before the Lamb, having each one a harp, and golden bowls full of incense which are the prayers of the saints. . . . And another angel came and stood at the altar, holding a golden censer; and much incense was given to him, that he might add it to the prayers of all the saints upon the golden altar which was before the throne. And the smoke of the incense, with the prayers of the saints, went up before God out of the angel's hand. And the angel took the censor; and he filled it with the fire of the altar and threw it to the earth; and there followed peals of thunder and sounds and flashing of lightning and an earthquake" (Revelation 5:8; 8:3-5, NASB).

According to these verses, either when He knows it is the right time to do something or when enough prayer has accumulated to get the job done, He releases power. He takes the bowl and mixes it with fire from the altar. . . . He mixes your bowl of prayers with His fire! Then He pours it upon earth.[5]

Understanding these truths about the power of our persistent intercession should give us confidence to remain faithful in prayer, and to encourage others to do the same.

Learning from the Holy Spirit

Before Jesus left this earth, He promised His followers, "I will ask the Father, and He will give you another Comforter (Counselor, Helper, Intercessor, Advocate, Strengthener, and Standby), that He may remain with you forever—the Spirit of Truth. . . . He will teach you all things" (John 14:16-17,26, *AMP*).

The Holy Spirit, our helper, teaches us to pray and strengthens us for battle. He testifies of Jesus, guides, reveals, comforts, imparts joy, gives spiritual gifts, liberates, empowers for service, and intercedes for us. Paul describes how the Holy Spirit also prays through us:

> In the same way, the Spirit helps us in our weakness. We do not know what we ought to pray for, but the Spirit himself intercedes for us with groans that words cannot express. And he who searches our hearts knows the mind of the Spirit, because the Spirit intercedes for the saints in accordance with God's will (Romans 8:26-27).

Interceding according to the will of God is a key principle for successful prayer. Many people believe that the Holy Spirit intercedes through us by praying in an unknown tongue. Bible teacher Judson Cornwall says, "Prayer is the most valuable use of tongues for it is 'speaking to God.'" He goes on to explain:

> The Holy Spirit is certainly not limited to the English language nor is He confined to modern languages. He has access to every language ever used by mankind, and He is very familiar with the language used in heaven. When deep intercession is needed, the Spirit often uses a language that is beyond the intellectual grasp of the speaker to bypass the censorship of his or her conscious mind, thereby enabling the Spirit to say what needs to be prayed without arguing with the faith level of the one through whom the intercession flows.[6]

This gift of praying in an unknown tongue is available to all born-again Christians, not just those who lived in the first century after Christ. As a child of God, all you need to do is ask for the gift Jesus promised (see John 14:16-17,26).

Scriptures on the Holy Spirit

These signs will accompany those who believe: In my name they will drive out demons; they will speak in new tongues (Mark 16:17).

Which of you fathers, if your son asks for a fish, will give him a snake instead? Or if he asks for an egg, will give him a scorpion? If you then, though you are evil, know how to give good gifts to your children, how much more will your Father in heaven give the Holy Spirit to those who ask him! (Luke 11:11-13).

You will receive power when the Holy Spirit comes on you; and you will be my witnesses in Jerusalem, and in all Judea and Samaria, and to the ends of the earth (Acts 1:8).

All of them [the 120 in the Upper Room] were filled with the Holy Spirit and began to speak in other tongues as the Spirit enabled them (Acts 2:4).

After they prayed, the place where they were meeting was shaken. And they were all filled with the Holy Spirit and spoke the word of God boldly (Acts 4:31).

God anointed Jesus of Nazareth with the Holy Spirit and power, and . . . he went around doing good and healing all who were under the power of the devil, because God was with him (Acts 10:38).

When Paul placed his hands on them, the Holy Spirit came on them, and they spoke in tongues and prophesied (Acts 19:6).

For anyone who speaks in a tongue does not speak to men but to God (1 Corinthians 14:2).

For if I pray in a tongue, my spirit prays, but my mind is unfruitful. So what shall I do? I will pray with my spirit, but I will also pray with my mind; I will sing with my spirit, but I will also sing with my mind (1 Corinthians 14:14-15).

You, dear friends, build yourselves up in your most holy faith and pray in the Holy Spirit (Jude 20).

Scriptures on Intercession

When you pray, go into your room, close the door and pray to your Father, who is unseen. Then your Father, who sees what is done in secret, will reward you. And when you pray, do not keep on babbling like pagans, for they think they will be heard because of their many words. Do not be like them, for your Father knows what you need before you ask him (Matthew 6:6-8).

Therefore, since we have a great high priest who has gone through the heavens, Jesus the Son of God, let us hold firmly to the faith we profess. For we do not have a high priest who is unable to sympathize with our weaknesses, but we have one who has been tempted in every way, just as we are—yet was without sin. Let us then approach the throne of grace with confidence, so that we may receive mercy and find grace to help us in our time of need (Hebrews 4:14-16).

Come near to God and he will come near to you. Wash your hands, you sinners, and purify your hearts, you double-minded. . . . Confess your sins to each other and pray for each other so that you may be healed. The prayer of a righteous man is powerful and effective (James 4:8; 5:16).

Prayer for Lost Loved Ones

Lord, thank You that it is not Your will that my loved ones perish. Please send people across their path who can share the Gospel message

*with power and conviction. God, grant them repentance,
leading to a personal relationship with Jesus. I stand against the forces
of darkness that are blinding them and holding them back, in the
name of Jesus. I tear down every stronghold of deception keeping them
in the enemy's camp. [Ask the Holy Spirit to reveal more
strongholds you may need to address.]*

*In Jesus' name and by His authority, these loved ones
[name them] are coming out of the kingdom of darkness and into
the kingdom of light. Lord, overwhelm them with Your grace; reveal
to them how much You love them and desire to set them free.
Thank You, Lord, that Your plan and purpose for them will prevail.
They will be saved! Amen.*

BATTLING AGAINST DECEPTION

Satan is a master of deception, as we can observe in the following examples. First he deceived himself in heaven: "I will raise my throne above the stars of God; I will sit enthroned on the mount of assembly, . . . I will ascend above the tops of the clouds; I will make myself like the Most High" (Isaiah 14:13-14).

Then he deceived Eve in the garden: " 'You will not surely die,' the serpent said. . . . 'When you eat of it your eyes will be opened, and you will be like God' " (Genesis 3:4-5).

He tried to deceive Jesus in the wilderness: "The devil led him up to a high place and showed him in an instant all the kingdoms of the world. And he said to him, 'So if you worship me, it will all be yours' " (Luke 4:5-7).

He succeeded in deceiving Judas in the Upper Room: "The evening meal was being served, and the devil had already prompted Judas . . . to betray Jesus. As soon as Judas took the bread, Satan entered into him" (John 13:2,27).

Jesus' prayer prevented him from succeeding with Peter: "Simon, Satan has asked to sift you as wheat. But I have prayed for you, Simon, that your faith may not fail" (Luke 22:31-32).

Are we susceptible as well? Absolutely!

Easy Prey for Deception

Because of the predisposition to sin with which we are born, all of us are easy prey for deception if our spiritual armor is not firmly in place. We can be deceived by the devil or his emissaries. We can be deceived by the seduction and smooth talk of others. We can be deceived by our own pride, selfishness and greed. God continually warned His people against being deceived into worshiping the false gods of surrounding nations:

> Be careful, or you will be enticed to turn away and worship other gods and bow down to them. Then the LORD's anger will burn against you. If your very own brother, or your son or daughter, or the wife you love, or your closest friend secretly entices you, saying, "Let us go and worship other gods," . . . do not yield to him or listen to him (Deuteronomy 11:16-17; 13:6,8).

To be deceived simply means to believe a lie instead of the truth. Deception always contains a grain of truth, just enough to make it *seem* believable, but enough to create confusion in the minds of many. However, truth and error cannot mix, just as iron and clay cannot mix.

The fall of Adam and Eve presents a classic case of deception. Various translations of Genesis 3:1 refer to the serpent as being clever, crafty, subtle and cunning. He is a master charlatan. Bible scholar E. W. Bullinger writes:

> The fall of man had to do solely with the Word of God, and is centered in the sin of believing Satan's lie instead of Jehovah's truth.
>
> The temptation of "the first man Adam" began with the question "Hath God said?" The temptation of "the second man, the Lord from heaven" began with the similar question, "If Thou be the Son of God," when the voice of the Father had scarcely died away which said "This is My beloved Son."
>
> All turned on the truth of what Jehovah had said. . . . Wherever the Word of God is called in question, there we see the trail of "that old serpent, which is the Devil, and Satan."[1]

We can almost feel Paul's pain when we read: "For Demas, because he loved this world, has deserted me" (2 Timothy 4:10). Most of us have suffered the pain of seeing another believer whom we know and love fall into deception of one kind or another. Those in positions of responsibility are often a likely target: intercessors, Bible teachers, pastors, worship leaders, missionaries, and elders and leaders in a congregation.

Some just lose their zeal for the Lord and become occasional pew sitters who represent no threat to the kingdom of darkness. Others fall into immorality or false doctrine and become an active reproach to the Body of Christ. A few actually forsake God completely.

How does deception happen? It all begins with entertaining Satan's suggestive question, "Did God really say?" When a person begins to doubt God's Word, soon that individual begins to believe his or her case is somehow different. It becomes easier for that person to rationalize sin. Some people even buy into the notion that if they do good works for God, He will excuse their sin.

Once a person believes the first lie, a host of others can march in unchallenged. We must all heed Paul's warning: "If you think you are standing firm, be careful that you don't fall!" (1 Corinthians 10:12). Paul also warned that "Satan himself masquerades as an angel of light" (2 Corinthians 11:14).

Old Testament Scriptures on Deceit

Now the serpent was more crafty than any of the wild animals the LORD God had made. He said to the woman, "Did God really say, 'You must not eat from any tree in the garden'?" The woman said to the serpent, "We may eat fruit from the trees in the garden, but God did say, 'You must not eat fruit from the tree that is in the middle of the garden, and you must not touch it, or you will die.'" "You will not surely die," the serpent said to the woman (Genesis 3:1-4).

Blessed is the man whose sin the LORD does not count against him and in whose spirit is no deceit (Psalm 32:2).

Do not withhold your mercy from me, O LORD; may your love and your truth always protect me (Psalm 40:11).

No one who practices deceit will dwell in my house; no one who speaks falsely will stand in my presence (Psalm 101:7).

Truthful lips endure forever, but a lying tongue lasts only a moment. There is deceit in the hearts of those who plot evil, but joy for those who promote peace (Proverbs 12:19-20).

Like a coating of glaze over earthenware are fervent lips with an evil heart. A malicious man disguises himself with his lips, but in his heart he harbors deceit. Though his speech is charming, do not believe him, for seven abominations fill his heart (Proverbs 26:23-25).

"You live in the midst of deception; in their deceit they refuse to acknowledge me," declares the LORD. Therefore this is what the LORD Almighty says: "See, I will refine and test them, for what else can I do because of the sin of my people?" (Jeremiah 9:6-7).

Warnings of Jesus

During His teaching ministry, Jesus said more than 80 times, "I tell you the truth." He knew the truth would protect His followers from error. His strongest warning concerning the end time was to "be not deceived" (Luke 21:8, *KJV*).

Watch out for false prophets. They come to you in sheep's clothing, but inwardly they are ferocious wolves. By their fruit you will recognize them. . . . A good tree cannot bear bad fruit, and a bad tree cannot bear good fruit (Matthew 7:15-16,18).

Watch out that no one deceives you. For many will come in my name, claiming, "I am the Christ," and will deceive many. . . . For false Christs and false prophets will appear and perform great signs and miracles to deceive even the elect—if that were possible (Matthew 24:4-5,24).

If you hold to my teaching, you are really my disciples. Then you will know the truth, and the truth will set you free (John 8:31-32).

Teachings of the Apostles

The law was given through Moses; grace and truth came through Jesus Christ (John 1:17).

Although they claimed to be wise, they became fools and exchanged the glory of the immortal God for images. . . . They exchanged the truth of God for a lie, and worshiped and served created things rather than the Creator (Romans 1:22-25).

As it is written: "There is no one righteous, not even one. . . . Their throats are open graves; their tongues practice deceit. . . . There is no fear of God before their eyes" (Romans 3:10,13,18).

I urge you, brothers, to watch out for those who cause divisions and put obstacles in your way that are contrary to the teaching you have learned. Keep away from them. . . . By smooth talk and flattery they deceive the minds of naive people (Romans 16:17-18).

Do not be deceived: Neither the sexually immoral nor idolaters nor adulterers nor male prostitutes nor homosexual offenders nor thieves nor the greedy nor drunkards nor slanderers nor swindlers will inherit the kingdom of God (1 Corinthians 6:9-10).

Let no one deceive you with empty words, for because of such things God's wrath comes on those who are disobedient. Therefore do not be partners with them (Ephesians 5:6).

See to it that no one takes you captive through hollow and deceptive philosophy, which depends on human tradition and the basic principles of this world rather than on Christ (Colossians 2:8).

If anyone teaches false doctrines and does not agree to the sound instruction of our Lord Jesus Christ and to godly teaching, he is conceited and understands nothing. He has an unhealthy interest in controversies and quarrels about words that result in envy, strife, malicious talk, evil suspicions and constant friction between men of corrupt mind, who have been robbed of the truth and who think that godliness is a means to financial gain (1 Timothy 6:3-5).

For the time will come when men will not put up with sound doctrine. Instead, to suit their own desires, they will gather around them a great number of teachers to say what their itching ears want to hear. They will turn their ears away from the truth and turn aside to myths (2 Timothy 4:3-4).

Each one is tempted when, by his own evil desire, he is dragged away and enticed. Then, after desire has conceived, it gives birth to sin; and sin, when it is full-grown, gives birth to death (James 1:14-15).

Christ suffered for you, leaving you an example, that you should follow in his steps. "He committed no sin, and no deceit was found in his mouth" (1 Peter 2:21-22).

If we claim to be without sin, we deceive ourselves and the truth is not in us (1 John 1:8).

Prayer

O Lord, how easy it is to be deceived! Father, forgive me for the times in the past when I failed to heed that still, small voice of warning. Help me to walk in Your ways and listen to and obey Your voice. Keep me from error, Lord, and help me to understand and apply the truth of Your Word. May I continually put my trust in You to guide and direct me, I pray in Jesus' name, amen.

25

STANDING AGAINST VERBAL ATTACK

Who among us has not been harassed by a neighbor, a relative or someone in authority over us? Who hasn't felt betrayed by a friend? Or unfairly treated or falsely accused by a teacher, a supervisor or even a church leader? Some of us have even been targets of unfounded lawsuits.

Perhaps you can identify with David's words: "Even my close friend, whom I trusted, he who shared my bread, has lifted up his heel against me" (Psalm 41:9). Certainly Jesus could. Just think: He knew beforehand that Judas, one of His inner circle of friends, would betray Him (see Matthew 26:46).

Yet even He who was betrayed gave us a noble example of how we should respond to our enemies: "You have heard that it was said, 'Love your neighbor and hate your enemy.' But I tell you: Love your enemies and pray for those who persecute you, that you may be sons of your Father in heaven" (Matthew 5:43-45). "And when you stand praying, if you hold anything against anyone, forgive him, so that your Father in heaven may forgive you your sins" (Mark 11:25).

Jesus took care to warn His followers about difficulties they would face: "I have told you these things, so that in me you may have peace. In this world you will have trouble. But take heart! I have overcome the world" (John 16:33).

The apostle Paul learned this lesson well. He wrote: "For Christ's sake, I delight in weaknesses, in insults, in hardships, in persecutions, in difficulties. For when I am weak, then I am strong" (2 Corinthians 12:10).

Let's examine some biblical examples of harassment or false accusation to strengthen our own spiritual battles against persecution.

Turning the Tables

In the book of Esther we read of Haman, who plotted to have the Jews within the Persian Empire annihilated. But Queen Esther called the Jewish people to fast and pray with her for their protection. When she risked her life by presenting herself to the king without having been called, he gave her favor and listened to her plea. Through a series of events that only God could have orchestrated, Haman's wicked conspiracy backfired: "When the plot came to the king's attention, he issued written orders that the evil scheme Haman had devised against the Jews should come back onto his own head, and that he and his sons should be hanged on the gallows" (Esther 9:25).

While Nehemiah was busy rebuilding the broken wall around Jerusalem, he was continually harassed by Sanballat and his cohorts, who did everything to stop the work. But Nehemiah prayed for God's strength and refused to negotiate with his enemies. The result? "The wall was completed . . . in fifty-two days. When all our enemies heard about this, all the surrounding nations were afraid and lost their self-confidence, because they realized that this work had been done with the help of our God" (Nehemiah 6:15-16).

The life of Joseph reveals a litany of betrayals and false accusations by those close to him—from his own brothers to his slave-master's wife to his fellow prisoners. This young man must have felt completely deserted, but somehow he resisted giving in to bitterness. Eventually God rescued him and showered him with favor. Joseph became prime minister of Egypt, the land of his exile.

When the same brothers who had betrayed him came to Egypt asking for food, Joseph showed no malice. He was able to say to them: "Do not be distressed and do not be angry with yourselves for selling me here. . . . God sent me ahead of you to preserve for you a remnant on earth and to save your lives by a great deliverance" (Genesis 45:5-7).

Not only does God come to our rescue when we are harassed, but also because we belong to Him, His favor shines upon us. You may feel you have been misunderstood and never had your name or reputation cleared. But God is the One who keeps the records, and He alone can vindicate us.

When we turn to our heavenly Father for strength and wisdom in the midst of verbal attack, He will enable us to love our enemies and pray for them. Who knows? Perhaps the verbal attack is the very crack in the door through which Jesus can enter your accuser's heart. Seize the opportunity to do spiritual battle for the Lord.

Take courage from this declaration Joseph made to his brothers: "As far as I am concerned, God turned into good what you meant for evil, for he brought me to this high position I have today so that I could save the lives of many people" (Genesis 50:20, *TLB*).

Scriptures on Seeing God as Vindicator

He rescued me from my powerful enemy, from my foes, who were too strong for me (Psalm 18:17).

Though they plot evil against you and devise wicked schemes, they cannot succeed (Psalm 21:11).

Teach me your way, O LORD; lead me in a straight path because of my oppressors. Do not turn me over to the desire of my foes, for false witnesses rise up against me, breathing out violence (Psalm 27:11-12).

How great is your goodness, which you have stored up for those who fear you, which you bestow in the sight of men on those who take refuge in you. In the shelter of your presence you hide them from the intrigues of men; in your dwelling you keep them safe from accusing tongues (Psalm 31:19-20).

You are my hiding place; you will protect me from trouble and surround me with songs of deliverance (Psalm 32:7).

Those who look to him are radiant; their faces are never covered with shame (Psalm 34:5).

Contend, O LORD, with those who contend with me; fight against those who fight against me. Take up shield and buckler; arise and come to my aid (Psalm 35:1-2).

For the LORD will vindicate his people and have compassion on his servants (Psalm 135:14).

For the LORD . . . holds victory in store for the upright, he is a shield to those whose walk is blameless, for he guards the course of the just and protects the way of his faithful ones (Proverbs 2:6-8).

There are six things the LORD hates, seven that are detestable to him: haughty eyes, a lying tongue, hands that shed innocent blood, a heart that devises wicked schemes, feet that are quick to rush into evil, a false witness who pours out lies and a man who stirs up dissension among brothers (Proverbs 6:16-19).

"No weapon forged against you will prevail, and you will refute every tongue that accuses you. This is the heritage of the servants of the LORD, and this is their vindication from me," declares the LORD (Isaiah 54:17).

If your enemy is hungry, feed him; if he is thirsty, give him something to drink. In doing this, you will heap burning coals on his head (Romans 12:20).

Live such good lives among the pagans that, though they accuse you of doing wrong, they may see your good deeds and glorify God on the day he visits us (1 Peter 2:12).

Scriptures on Receiving God's Favor

While Joseph was there in the prison, the LORD was with him; he showed him kindness and granted him favor in the eyes of the prison warden (Genesis 39:20-21).

Moses sought the favor of the LORD his God. . . . "If you are pleased with me, teach me your ways so I may know you and continue to find favor with you. Remember that this nation is your people" (Exodus 32:11; 33:13).

I will look on you with favor and make you fruitful and increase your numbers, and I will keep my covenant with you (Leviticus 26:9).

For the LORD God is a sun and shield; the LORD bestows favor and honor; no good thing does he withhold from those whose walk is blameless (Psalm 84:11).

For whoever finds me [Wisdom] finds life and receives favor from the LORD (Proverbs 8:35).

This is what the LORD says: "In the time of my favor I will answer you, and in the day of salvation I will help you; I will keep you and will make you to be a covenant for the people" (Isaiah 49:8).

Now God had caused the official to show favor and sympathy to Daniel. . . . To these four young men God gave knowledge and understanding of all kinds of literature and learning. And Daniel could understand visions and dreams of all kinds (Daniel 1:9,17).

"The Lord has done this for me," she [Mary] said. "In these days he has shown his favor and taken away my disgrace among the people." But the angel said to her, "Do not be afraid, Mary, you have found favor with God" (Luke 1:25,30).

And Jesus grew in wisdom and stature, and in favor with God and men (Luke 2:52).

Prayer Against Harassment or False Accusation

Father, thank You that no tongue speaking against me shall do me permanent harm. My reputation, my life is in Your hands. My hope is in You, Lord—You are my defender, my stronghold and my deliverer. I trust You to reveal truth and to bestow favor upon me. I trust You to cause what the enemy means for evil to be turned to good. Father, I ask that You do the maximum to glorify Your Son as You bring resolution to these circumstances, in Jesus' name, amen!

26

PRAYING FOR SPIRITUAL LEADERS

We can learn much about effective spiritual warfare by studying accounts of battles in the natural realm. For example, the general who devises superior strategy usually defeats his enemy. History is full of examples of such successful strategists. If a military general can somehow weaken the resolve of the leaders of the opposing forces, his side is much more likely to win the conflict.

We see these principles paralleled in the supernatural realm. Consider this observation by William Gurnall:

> Two periods stand out in Christ's life: his entrance into public ministry at his baptism, and the culmination of it at his passion. At both he had a fierce encounter with the devil. This should give you an idea of how the master tempter works. . . . The more eminent your service for God, the greater the probability that Satan is at that very moment hatching some deadly scheme against you. If even the cadet corps need to be armed against Satan's bullets of temptation, how much more the commanders and officers, who stand in the front line of battle![1]

Scripture warns all believers: "Be self-controlled and alert. Your enemy the devil prowls around like a roaring lion looking for someone to devour" (1 Peter 5:8). Christians need to be constantly vigilant against spiritual attack on themselves or their loved ones. But those in positions of leadership sorely need our prayer support as well. Dr. C. Peter Wagner warns, "If he [the devil] has a choice, he will devour a leader before he will devour anyone else. And he will use every weapon in his arsenal to do it."[2]

The apostle Paul requested personal intercession in his letters five times. He valued it; indeed, he counted on it:

> I urge you, brothers, by our Lord Jesus Christ and by the love of the Spirit, to join me in my struggle by praying to God for me (Romans 15:30).

> On him [God] we have set our hope that he will continue to deliver us, as you help us by your prayers. Then many will give thanks on our behalf for the gracious favor granted us in answer to the prayers of many (2 Corinthians 1:10-11).

> Pray also for me, that whenever I open my mouth, words may be given me so that I will fearlessly make known the mystery of the gospel (Ephesians 6:19).

Spiritual Leaders Need Intercessors

Because of their high visibility and influence, Christian pastors and other leaders need intercession even more than ordinary members of the Body of Christ. The enemy targets those in leadership because he knows that when a leader falls, it results in disillusionment, confusion and division (see Mark 14:27). Immature Christians may give up their faith entirely, while more mature believers often struggle with unforgiveness and bitterness. Joy Dawson, who for decades has taught principles of intercession, writes this:

> Leadership responsibility brings great privilege and accountability. James 3:1 makes it clear that because of the enormous influence they exert, teachers are judged by God with greater strictness. Teachers reproduce their own kind, and God doesn't want to multiply phonies. However, it's part of God's justice that spiritual leaders get more prayer support than others because of their additional responsibility and accountability.
>
> When we perceive that a spiritual leader is in error, or has failed to meet our expectations, as a general rule, let us adopt the slogan, "Don't say it; pray it." Talk to the One who can

correct the problem, not to the ones who could spread it. . . . For our prayers to be effective we must have a forgiving spirit and a loving heart.[3]

Intercessors Need Safeguards

Some pastors are wary of allowing intercessory prayer groups to function in the church because of potential problems or because of a negative experience they've had in the past. Of course the enemy will try to incite trouble in order to discredit the value of intercession. But the wise pastor will establish prayer as an important priority by his or her own example and set up safeguards to prevent imbalance, lack of wisdom or excessive zeal in the prayer group.

Once in a while an individual who prays in a selfish or controlling way or who prays with impure motives will join an intercessors' group. Cindy Jacobs, in her book *Possessing the Gates of the Enemy*, describes these people as "flaky intercessors":

> Men and women who for a variety of reasons, drift outside biblical guidelines in their zeal for prayer. They bring reproach on their ministries and confusion and division in the church. . . . Many aspiring intercessors pray out of bitterness and woundedness. What I find remarkable is that they are unaware of these heart conditions. They are drawn to intercession because of its great power and, subconsciously, because they see it as a means of getting their way. . . . A good prayer for intercessors, therefore, is "Lord, show me my heart so that I can remain pure before you always."[4]

Missionaries and Gospel Workers Need Prayer

Missionaries and gospel workers are leaders by virtue of their tasks, so they also need our prayers. Pray that God will send angels to watch over them in their travels (see Psalm 91) and that He will make a hedge to protect their family, property and possessions.

1. Pray that the Lord will send angels before them to do battle on their behalf (see Psalm 78:49).

2. Pray that all attacks and traps of the enemy will be foiled, and the workers will be kept from the nets of the enemy while they walk by safely (see Psalm 141:9-10).

3. Pray that God will be their "hiding place" and preserve them "from trouble," surrounding them "with songs of deliverance" (Psalm 32:7).

4. Pray that they will be sensitivite to the Holy Spirit and that they will have "the spirit of wisdom and revelation" (Ephesians 1:17).

5. Pray that the Word of God will go forth as a double-edged sword, judging the attitudes and thoughts of the hearts of the hearers (see Hebrews 4:12).

6. Pray that the workers will be anointed "to preach good news to the poor . . . to bind up the brokenhearted, to proclaim freedom for the captives and release from darkness for the prisoners" (Isaiah 61:1).

7. Pray that the Word will fall on hearts open to hear and obey the Lord (see Luke 8:15), and that the enemy will not steal the Word after it is sown (see Luke 8:12).

Leaders Are Vulnerable Targets

The media love to report alleged scandals and failures in the lives of high-profile ministers and televangelists. In addition, probably every person who reads this book knows personally one or more spiritual leaders who have fallen into the enemy's trap of moral failure. Especially when a leader takes a tumble, the diligent spiritual warrior should continue to pray for that individual and for all the people affected by the tragedy.

On the heels of such a fiasco, the devil works on those who feel hurt, betrayed or disappointed, tempting them to give in to cynicism and bitterness. But the true intercessor will stand in the gap against Satan's attempts to destroy the faith of the wounded ones. He or she will also cry out to God for the fallen leader's restoration. No matter how devastating a situation seems to be, the persistent prayer warrior affirms that God can take what the devil meant for evil and turn it to good (see Genesis 50:20).

Several other sections of this book—especially chapter 24, "Battling Against Deception"—provide guidelines and Scriptures to pray for leaders. Use the sword of the Spirit and the weapons of the blood of Jesus and praise to push back Satan's assaults against those in spiritual authority.

Samuel Was a Mighty Intercessor

The prophet Samuel is an example of an intercessor who prayed for a nation and for its leader. On one occasion the Israelites heard that the Philistines had assembled and were going to attack them. They begged Samuel, "Do not stop crying out to the LORD our God for us, that he may rescue us from the hand of the Philistines" (1 Samuel 7:8).

Later Israel demanded—against God's plan—that Samuel appoint a king to rule over them. The prophet knew their sin of rebellion meant trouble. But he wisely informed them: "As for me, far be it from me that I should sin against the LORD by failing to pray for you" (1 Samuel 12:23).

On another occasion, Samuel agonized over Saul's disobedience: "Then Samuel went home to Ramah, and Saul returned to his house at Gibeah. Samuel never went to meet with Saul again, but he mourned constantly for him. And the LORD was sorry he had ever made Saul king of Israel" (1 Samuel 15:34-35, NLT). Samuel was faithful to pray for this fallen leader, even when Saul refused to heed the prophet's warnings or to repent for his sin.

Scriptures

Then the word of the LORD came to Samuel: "I am grieved that I have made Saul king, because he has turned away from me and has not carried out my instructions." Samuel was troubled, and he cried out to the LORD all that night (1 Samuel 15:10-11).

May my heart be blameless toward your decrees, that I may not be put to shame (Psalm 119:80).

He whose walk is blameless is kept safe, but he whose ways are perverse will suddenly fall (Proverbs 28:18).

Pray in the Spirit on all occasions with all kinds of prayers and requests. With this in mind, be alert and always keep on praying for all the saints (Ephesians 6:18).

I thank my God every time I remember you. In all my prayers for all of you, I always pray with joy because of your partnership in the gospel from the first day until now, being confident of this, that he who began a good work in you will carry it on to completion until the day of Christ Jesus (Philippians 1:3-6).

We always thank God for all of you, mentioning you in our prayers (1 Thessalonians 1:2).

May he strengthen your hearts so that you will be blameless and holy in the presence of our God and Father when our Lord Jesus comes with all his holy ones (1 Thessalonians 3:13).

May God himself, the God of peace, sanctify you through and through. May your whole spirit, soul and body be kept blameless at the coming of our Lord Jesus Christ (1 Thessalonians 5:23).

An elder must be blameless, the husband of but one wife, a man whose children believe and are not open to the charge of being wild and disobedient. Since an overseer is entrusted with God's work, he must be blameless—not overbearing, not quick-tempered, not given to drunkenness, not violent, not pursuing dishonest gain (Titus 1:6-7).

I always thank my God as I remember you in my prayers. . . . I pray that you may be active in sharing your faith, so that you will have a full understanding of every good thing we have in Christ (Philemon 4-6).

So then, dear friends, since you are looking forward to this [the day of the Lord], make every effort to be found spotless, blameless and at peace with him (2 Peter 3:14).

Prayer for a Pastor

In his book *Preyed On or Prayed For*, Dr. Terry Tekyl suggests numerous ways to pray for spiritual leaders. Here is his idea for praying Psalm 23 for your pastor:

> *The Lord is my pastor's shepherd; he or she will lack no good thing.*
> *You, Lord, give my pastor rest. Restore my pastor's energy.*
> *Guide my pastor in the paths of righteousness for your name's sake.*
> *Let no fear come near the parsonage. Comfort and anoint him or her,*
> *and let my pastor's cup overflow! And Lord, as a church we are in*
> *agreement that goodness and mercy will follow our pastor*
> *everywhere, and he or she will richly dwell in your presence. Amen.*[5]

MOBILIZING PRAYER GROUPS

In ancient times, soldiers served as watchmen on the wall. Keeping guard over a city was absolutely essential to the safety of the inhabitants. These soldiers were the "early warning system" for the armies of that era.

Today's intercessors serve as the modern counterpart to watchmen. In the spiritual realm, they serve as the radar system for the Body of Christ. Within the ranks of church congregations, intercessors are mobilizing into prayer groups in increasing numbers. They meet to pray for their leaders, for the congregation, for their communities, and for whatever is on God's heart when they come together.

Watchmen must be mentally alert, observant, vigilant. They guard and protect and remain attentive to the enemy's schemes to ward them off or to warn others about what is happening. They remain constantly on the lookout during their watch, or assigned shift. In biblical times watchmen were positioned not only on the city wall but also in a watchtower—located either in a field or a vineyard. Jamie Buckingham parallels these towers with our own situation:

> The watchtower was a familiar sight in Jesus' day. Built of the stones taken from a field, it usually sat in the middle of a field or a vineyard. . . . At night the watchmen would take turns during various "watches" of the night to guard the field—protecting it from foxes, bears, and poachers.
>
> In Old Testament days these towers were used by military watchmen. The soldiers would be looking out for the Philistines, fierce bands of renegades who would wait until the

crops were ripe, then swoop down to harvest what another man
had cultivated. . . .

You may not think your little field is very important. But
God has set you in your field as a watchman. Each one of us has
a sphere of influence. Most of us don't realize it, but our influence is much larger than we can ever imagine—and will continue
on for generations to come, be it good or evil. It's a wonderful
responsibility—frightening at times—but wonderful. Always remember, though, you're never in your watchtower alone. Jesus
is ever with you, and his Spirit will whisper just the things you
need to say and do.[1]

Take your places as watchmen in the tower where God has placed
you, confident that as you focus your trust upon Him, He will direct
your intercession to hit the target.

Guidelines for Mobilizing Prayer Groups

Rallying groups of intercessors to pray in agreement for a given area of responsibility is a powerful way to influence families, congregations, neighborhoods, cities and entire regions.[2] We are familiar with one church that
has more than 20 prayer groups, each with a special prayer assignment.
These groups pray for the senior pastor, other staff pastors, the children's
and youth ministries, evangelism outreaches, missionaries supported by
the church, unreached people groups, the church's Christian school, plus
many other areas of ministry. Once a month a prayer leader calls for vol-
unteers to prayerwalk a specific area of the community.

For such a prayer effort to work well, a prayer pastor or designated
individual needs to coordinate the planning of the various prayer groups
and communicate regularly with the leaders. How do you identify a
good leader? These are some key characteristics to look for:

- A teachable spirit with a willingness to serve
- The ability to work well with others
- A zeal for prayer and compassion for the lost
- The willingness and means to communicate effectively
- Discernment and sensitivity toward others
- The ability to inspire and lead others without being controlling

We suggest the following guidelines for the one who takes the responsibility to lead a prayer session or group:

- Prepare yourself in prayer and in Scripture-reading ahead of the meeting.
- Ask the Lord to reveal to you the prayer that is on His heart for this session. It is good to prepare prayer points in advance, but it's important to be sensitive to the Holy Spirit's leading.
- Be open to a variety of ways for prayers to be expressed. These could include prayers of petition, Scripture praying, proclamation prayers, praise and worship, repenting on behalf of a person or group that you are interceding for, laying hands on a person in the group needing prayer, or praying prayers of agreement for those needing prayer who aren't present.
- Ask participants to be in agreement with the one praying at a given moment, while also remaining sensitive to God's leading concerning the general flow of the meeting. When you sense the Lord directing you to switch to another prayer focus, let the group know it is time to make that shift.
- Encourage everyone to participate who feels led to speak or pray aloud, but stress the need to allow time for others to take part as well. If some in the group are reluctant to pray aloud, include them by asking them to read a Scripture or to share what is on their hearts.
- Strive to begin and end the meeting on time to encourage punctuality. If some want to linger and continue praying after the usual closing time, take a break, so those who must leave can do so comfortably.

Calls for the Church to Pray

Once an intercessory prayer group is functioning within a church, the whole congregation usually becomes more aware of the importance of prayer. By providing specific guidelines for prayer each month, everyone can focus on the same prayer needs and greater results usually are seen. Here's an example:

For the Church

1. Continue to press into a position to hear God's voice (see Psalm 85:8). Pray for breakthroughs in the following areas:

   - Strengthening of marriages and families
   - Provision and favor for those who are seeking jobs
   - Release of our singles into fullness of opportunity in the kingdom of God
   - Healing and a hedge of physical protection around our church family
   - Encouragement and care of our senior citizens

2. Pray for the missionaries our church supports—especially for protection of those working in hostile nations and those having problems maintaining their visas.

For the State

Pray for our government leaders to make godly decisions in the following areas (see 1 Timothy 2:1-4):

   - Marriage laws and other issues affecting the stability of families
   - Abortion issues
   - Textbook selection for public schools
   - Freedom to express one's faith in public settings

For International Concerns

1. Pray for the nation of Israel (see Zechariah 2:8; Romans 10:1; 11:26). Pray that believers there will have greater influence upon the life of the nation and that the messianic leaders will be unified.

2. Pray for areas of the world where people are dealing with famine, civil war, brutal dictators, violence, or persecution against Christians.

Scriptures

So Joshua . . . chose thirty thousand of his best fighting men and sent them out at night with these orders: "Listen carefully. You are to set an ambush behind the city. Don't go very far from it. All of you be on the alert" (Joshua 8:3-4).

Give ear, O LORD, and hear;... listen to the words Sennacherib has sent to insult the living God. Now, O LORD our God, deliver from his hand, so that all kingdoms on earth may know that you alone ... are God (2 Kings 19:16,19).

The people of Judah came together to seek help from the LORD; indeed, they came from every town in Judah to seek him. Then Jehoshaphat stood up in the assembly of Judah and Jerusalem at the temple of the LORD in the front of the new courtyard and said: "... We have no power to face this vast army that is attacking us. We do not know what to do, but our eyes are upon you" (2 Chronicles 20:4-5,12).

You hear, O LORD, the desire of the afflicted; you encourage them, and you listen to their cry (Psalm 10:17).

I will instruct you and teach you in the way you should go; I will counsel you and watch over you (Psalm 32:8).

I have posted watchmen on your walls, O Jerusalem; they will never be silent day or night. You who call on the LORD, give yourselves no rest, and give him no rest till he establishes Jerusalem and makes her the praise of the earth (Isaiah 62:6-7).

If the watchman sees the sword coming and does not blow the trumpet to warn the people and the sword comes and takes the life of one of them, that man will be taken away because of his sin, but I will hold the watchman accountable for his blood. "Son of man, I have made you a watchman for the house of Israel; so hear the word I speak and give them warning from me" (Ezekiel 33:6-7).

Look at the nations and watch—and be utterly amazed. For I am going to do something in your days that you would not believe, even if you were told (Habakkuk 1:5).

I will stand at my watch and station myself on the ramparts; I will look to see what he will say to me, and what answer I am to give to this complaint (Habakkuk 2:1).

I will defend my house against marauding forces. Never again will an oppressor overrun my people, for now I am keeping watch (Zechariah 9:8).

Watch out for false prophets. They come to you in sheep's clothing, but inwardly they are ferocious wolves (Matthew 7:15).

Therefore keep watch, because you do not know on what day your Lord will come. But understand this: If the owner of the house had known at what time of night the thief was coming, he would have kept watch and would not have let his house be broken into (Matthew 24:42-43).

What I say to you, I say to everyone: "Watch!" (Mark 13:37).

Then he returned to his disciples and found them sleeping. "Simon," he said to Peter, "are you asleep? Could you not keep watch for one hour? Watch and pray so that you will not fall into temptation. The spirit is willing, but the body is weak" (Mark 14:37-38).

It will be good for those servants whose master finds them ready, even if he comes in the second or third watch of the night (Luke 12:38).

So then, let us not be like others, who are asleep, but let us be alert and self-controlled (1 Thessalonians 5:6).

Prayer

Father God, please connect me with the right prayer team, or give me clear direction and confirmation if it is Your will for me to organize a prayer group. Help me to make prayer and intercession a higher priority as I link up with other intercessors. Keep us alert and spiritually attuned to pray what is on Your heart. May we be focused watchmen, ready to pray anytime the Holy Spirit nudges us. Lord, be glorified through us as we are faithful to stand in the gap, in Jesus' name, amen.

PRAYING FOR YOUR NEIGHBORHOOD, CITY AND NATION

From the time He called Abraham and promised to make a nation of Him, God intended His people to be a means of blessing other nations of the earth. Note these verses:

> Abraham will surely become a great and powerful nation, and all nations on earth will be blessed through him (Genesis 18:18).

> "Seek the peace and prosperity of the city to which I have carried you into exile. Pray to the LORD for it, because if it prospers, you too will prosper.... For I know the plans I have for you," declares the LORD, "plans to prosper you and not to harm you, plans to give you hope and a future" (Jeremiah 29:7,11).

God exhorts all of us to pray for the peace and prosperity of the city and region where we live. He also directs individual intercessors to pray for cities and nations where our feet have never walked, for in prayer we can "possess the land" so that God's purposes can be fulfilled and the gospel proclaimed in those areas.

Spiritual warfare is required to tear down strongholds of deception and unbelief to enable people to hear and respond to the gospel—this is an essential element of evangelism. The apostle Paul wrote: "Even if our gospel is veiled, it is veiled to those who are perishing. The god of this age has blinded the minds of unbelievers, so that they cannot see the light of the gospel of the glory of Christ" (2 Corinthians 4:3-4). This is why intercessors are needed to stand in the gap!

Covering Your Neighborhood

In their book *Prayerwalking: Praying On-Site with Insight*, Steve Hawthorne and Graham Kendrick write:

> Prayer walking is just what it sounds like it would be: walking while praying. . . . Prayerwalking is on-site prayer—simply praying in the very places where you expect your prayers to be answered. . . . Walking helps sensitize you to the realities of your community. Sounds, sights and smells, far from distracting your prayer, engage both body and mind in the art of praying. Better perception means boosted intercession. . . . By regularly passing through the streets of their cities, walkers can present an easygoing accessibility to neighbors. Walking seems to create opportunities to help or to pray for new friends on the spot, right at the times of great need.[1]

Years ago, an intercessor in North Carolina began prayerwalking her neighborhood, and then she organized "prayer triplets"—three people praying together for their neighbors and community. She encourages women to intercede daily for their neighbors and to pray for God to raise up a prayer movement in each neighborhood. She takes literally Jesus' command to "love your neighbor as yourself" (Matthew 19:19; Mark 12:31; Luke 10:27) and the admonition to "declare the praises of him who called you out of darkness into his wonderful light" (1 Peter 2:9).

Walking on her street, she makes it a habit to proclaim Scripture: "Lord, we invite the King of Glory to come in. Come forth and bring Your glory into this neighborhood. Release Your blessing to the families here."

As you begin praying over your own neighborhood, no doubt the Holy Spirit will guide you to certain verses to pray and proclaim over your neighbors. Be open to opportunities to interact with the people you meet and let them know that they are in your prayers. People may be offended by witnessing they feel is too aggressive, but few will be upset by knowing a friend cares enough to pray for them.

Transforming Communities

One couple who wanted to see a halt to the mysterious murders in their small southern town decided to do something to end the enemy's rampage. With the approval of the sheriff's department and city council, they set up a neighborhood watch by inviting people from 90 homes near them to attend the initial meeting. Then eight block captains were appointed, most of them Christians.

Neighbors began to watch out for strangers or suspicious activity. Many block captains led their groups in prayer for the neighborhood. After three years of close watchfulness, they reported the results: Only one more murder occurred (and it was in a different part of town), children now felt safe to play in playgrounds again, residences had been spruced up, and women who formed closer friendships now prayed together regularly.

"Many neighborhoods across our nation have block parties at least once a year, where neighbors gather to get to know each other better," the wife reported. "But imagine the powerful results if more of them got together to pray for their neighborhood or each other. What the enemy meant for evil in our neighborhood, God has turned for good."

Could our communities be truly transformed by Christ if every neighbor and neighborhood were prayed for daily? Christians from numerous churches in one western city decided to do that one spring. The goal was for each participant or couple to pray blessings over five of their neighbors and to be available to them when needed. This is what they agreed to pray:

Five blessings for
Five neighbors for
Five minutes a day
Five days a week for
Five weeks.[2]

Each member of the congregations willing to participate took a sheet of instructions with these suggestions: Pray for five specific neighbors during your regular prayer time. Jesus described a neighbor as someone you meet along life's road who needs your help. Think of the word "bless" to remember the five important ways to pray for your neighbors:

B *Body*: health, protection, strength
L *Labor*: work, income, security
E *Emotions*: joy, peace, hope
S *Social*: love, marriage, family, friends
S *Spiritual*: salvation, faith, grace.[3]

Many in these congregations did not stop after the initial five weeks but continued their prayer coverage for years. They report that notable changes occurred in the lives and circumstances of some of those they prayed for.

Spiritual Mapping

"Spiritual mapping" is a term meaning to record, or map, the spiritual condition of a territory. God once instructed the prophet Ezekiel:

Take a large clay brick and set it down in front of you. Then draw a map of the city of Jerusalem on it. Show the city under siege. Build a wall around it so no one can escape. Set up the enemy camp, and surround the city with siege ramps and battering rams. Then take an iron griddle and place it between you and the city. Turn toward the city and demonstrate how harsh the siege will be against Jerusalem. This will be a warning to the people of Israel (Ezekiel 4:1-3, *NLT*).

Experienced intercessors interpret this passage to mean that Ezekiel was to engage in a spiritual warfare tactic by praying over the city—not going to war against it, but demonstrating how Jerusalem would be besieged if the people ignored the warnings God sent through the prophet.

Those who believe in spiritual mapping often do historical research concerning a given area of interest, looking for clues that will reveal the inroads Satan has used to infiltrate that territory. They also study its Christian history in an attempt to build upon what the forefathers of faith began, especially during times of revival. They may also pray over maps of the area or walk the streets in prayer groups, after appropriate orientation and preparation.

Researching a City

John Dawson, in *Taking Our Cities for God: How to Break Spiritual Strongholds,* talks about researching the particular city where you live. These are principles you can apply to cities or nations anywhere in the world. Note the relevant questions:

> Do you know your city? You should have the census in one hand and the Bible in the other. What percentage of people actually attend church? How many people are in poverty? Why are they in poverty? Where do they live? Are there subcultures, ethnic groups, changes in the economy, an aging problem? What's really going on? You need to know if you are going to help free your city from evil spiritual dominance.
>
> First, get out a map of the city. Study it carefully. See if you can identify concentrations of the elderly, the homeless, students, children and so on. What subcultures are more receptive than others to the gospel? Why? What are the felt needs of the people of the city? . . . Parts of the city may vary greatly in culture, crime levels and wealth. . . .
>
> What you research depends on your goals. A pastor planting a church or an evangelist planning an outreach will need very specific information and statistics. However, all of us are called to the ministry of intercession."[4]

One righteous man stood before God and interceded for the wicked city of Sodom (see Genesis 18:16-33). Abraham asked God if he would spare Sodom if he found 50 righteous people there. Yes. If only 45? Yes. If only 40? 30? 20? Finally, if there were only 10? God was willing. Yet the wicked city was destroyed—obviously for lack of righteousness. But who can say whether Sodom might have been spared if Abraham had persisted in his intercession? May we never give up the assignment of praying for our neighborhoods, cities and nation!

Scriptures

"I have seen these people," the LORD said to Moses, "and they are a stiff-necked people. Now leave me alone so that my anger may burn against them and that I may destroy them. Then I will make you into a great nation." But Moses sought the favor of the LORD his God. "O LORD," he said, "why should your anger burn against your people, whom you brought out of Egypt with great power and a mighty hand? . . . Turn from your fierce anger; relent and do not bring disaster on your people. Remember your servants Abraham, Isaac and Israel, to whom you swore by your own self: 'I will make your descendants as numerous as the stars in the sky and I will give your descendants all this land I promised them, and it will be their inheritance forever.'" Then the LORD relented and did not bring on his people the disaster he had threatened (Exodus 32:9-14).

If my people, who are called by my name, will humble themselves and pray and seek my face and turn from their wicked ways, then will I hear from heaven and will forgive their sin and will heal their land (2 Chronicles 7:14).

Ask of me, and I will make the nations your inheritance, the ends of the earth your possession (Psalm 2:8).

The LORD foils the plans of the nations; he thwarts the purposes of the peoples (Psalm 33:10).

I will praise you, O LORD, among the nations; I will sing of you among the peoples. For great is your love, reaching to the heavens; your faithfulness reaches to the skies. Be exalted, O God, above the heavens; let your glory be over all the earth (Psalm 57:9-11).

May God be gracious to us . . . that your ways may be known on earth, your salvation among all nations. May the peoples praise you, O God; may all the peoples praise you. May the nations be glad and sing for joy, for you rule the peoples justly and guide the nations of the earth (Psalm 67:1-4).

Woe to those who go down to Egypt for help, who rely on horses, who trust in the multitude of their chariots and in the great strength of their horsemen, but do not look to the Holy One of Israel, or seek help from the LORD. . . . The Egyptians are men and not God; their horses are flesh and not spirit. . . . At the thunder of your voice, the peoples flee; when you rise up, the nations scatter (Isaiah 31:1-3; 33:3).

Turn to me and be saved, all you ends of the earth; for I am God, and there is no other. By myself I have sworn, my mouth has uttered in all integrity a word that will not be revoked: Before me every knee will bow; by me every tongue will swear. They will say of me, "In the LORD alone are righteousness and strength." All who have raged against him will come to him and be put to shame (Isaiah 45:22-24).

See, today I appoint you over nations and kingdoms to uproot and tear down, to destroy and overthrow, to build and to plant (Jeremiah 1:10).

Many nations will come and say, "Come, let us go up to the mountain of the LORD, to the house of the God of Jacob. He will teach us his ways, so that we may walk in his paths." The law will go out from Zion, the word of the LORD from Jerusalem. He will judge between many peoples and will settle disputes for strong nations far and wide. They will beat their swords into plowshares and their spears into pruning hooks. Nation will not take up sword against nation, nor will they train for war anymore (Micah 4:2-3).

LORD, I have heard of your fame; I stand in awe of your deeds, O LORD. Renew them in our day, in our time make them known; in wrath remember mercy (Habakkuk 3:2).

"My name will be great among the nations, from the rising to the setting of the sun. In every place . . . my name will be great among the nations," says the LORD Almighty (Malachi 1:11).

"Ever since the time of your forefathers you have turned away from my decrees and have not kept them. Return to me, and I will return to you," says the LORD Almighty (Malachi 3:7).

Therefore God exalted him [Christ] to the highest place and gave him the name that is above every name, that at the name of Jesus every knee should bow, in heaven and on earth and under the earth, and every tongue confess that Jesus Christ is Lord, to the glory of God the Father (Philippians 2:9-11).

Who will not fear you, O Lord, and bring glory to your name? For you alone are holy. All nations will come and worship before you, for your righteous acts have been revealed (Revelation 15:4).

Prayer to Repent for a Region

Lord, we repent before You for the way the people of our [city, state, or nation] have veered from Your Word and broken Your commandments. We are truly sorry and ask for Your mercy and forgiveness. Help us to purify our hearts, abandon our wicked ways and walk in Your path. May we honor You in our nation and boldly declare, "In God we trust." We ask this in the name of our Savior, Jesus Christ, amen.

Prayer for Protection of Our Nation

Father God, we ask you to guard the borders and the entry points to our nation; our waterways, ship channels, ports and bridges; our border crossings and all transportation systems; our schools, colleges, libraries and stadiums; our hospital and medical facilities; our public office buildings, shopping complexes, banking institutions and postal system; our electrical and nuclear power plants; our gas and oil distribution centers; our military bases; our densely populated

*cities; our nation's capital; our churches and synagogues.
We pray protection over our president and his advisors, and over
Congress, judges, law enforcement and security personnel, and all
those in positions of authority. Lord, uncover any plots or planned
attacks against our nation that they may be swiftly exposed and
dismantled. Help us to be sensitive to the Holy Spirit's call to
intercede when prayer is needed. Thank You in advance, Lord,
for Your shield of protection over us, in Jesus' name, amen.*

Prayer for an Election

*Dear God, as our citizens exercise their freedom and responsibility to
vote in this election, grant us wisdom and discernment in the choices
we make. We pray that moral, God-fearing men and women will
find favor in local, state and national campaigns and be elected to
public office. Lord, show us Your will concerning the individuals and
issues presented on the ballot. We pray that truth will be revealed
and that corruption, immorality, hidden agendas or special interests
will be exposed. Lord, may this election take place peacefully as
eligible citizens of our community vote and as those working in the
polls do their jobs with honesty and excellence. Thank You, Lord,
for the freedoms You have granted us in this nation. Amen.*

EPILOGUE

Spiritual warfare is valuable and effective at a personal level. It works for yourself, your children, your household. But God's plan is much bigger. It is worldwide!

As we have seen throughout this book, even though Christ's decisive victory over Satan is complete, we need to do our part in enforcing that victory through prayer and spiritual warfare.

Each of us has a specific sphere of influence and a certain set of friends that no one else has. God puts them in our path for His divine purposes, one of which is for us to pray for one another and for the region where we live.

Ask God for your prayer assignment and don't give up! The only way we lose the battle is to quit. In times of weariness and discouragement, we must refocus on our commander, Jesus Christ, and draw our strength from Him. He is a mighty warrior!

> *Through God we will do valiantly, for it is He who*
> *shall tread down our enemies.*
> PSALM 108:13, NKJV

ENDNOTES

Chapter 1: Putting on the Armor

1. E. M. Bounds, *Winning the Invisible War* (Springdale, PA: Whitaker House, 1984), p. 24.
2. R. Arthur Mathews, *Born for Battle: 31 Studies on Spiritual Warfare* (Robesonia, PA: OMF Books, 1978), p. 54.
3. William Gurnall, *The Christian in Complete Armour*, vol. 1, abridged by Ruthanne Garlock, et al. (Carlisle, PA: Banner of Truth Trust, 1986), pp. 59, 65, 82.

Chapter 2: Taking Authority in the Name of Jesus

1. W. E. Vine, *Vine's Expository Dictionary of New Testament Words* (Old Tappan, NJ: Fleming H. Revell, 1981), p. 89.
2. Dean Sherman, *Spiritual Warfare for Every Christian: How to Live in Victory and Retake the Land* (Seattle, WA: Frontline Communications, 1990), p. 111. Used by permission of the author.
3. Ibid., p. 123.
4. J. Oswald Sanders, *Effective Prayer* (Singapore: OMF Books, 1961), p. 19.

Chapter 3: The Power of the Blood of Jesus

1. G. Campbell Morgan, *The Teaching of Christ* (Old Tappan, NJ: Fleming H. Revell Co., 1913), p. 254.
2. H. A. Maxwell Whyte, *The Power of the Blood* (Springdale, PA: Whitaker House, 1973), pp. 44, 78.
3. R. Arthur Mathews, *Born for Battle: 31 Studies on Spiritual Warfare* (Robesonia, PA: OMF Books, 1978), p. 63.

Chapter 4: The Power of the Word of God

1. William Gurnall, *The Christian in Complete Armour*, vol. 3, abridged by Ruthanne Garlock, et al. (Carlisle, PA: Banner of Truth Trust, 1989), pp. 244, 245, 247.
2. Roy Hicks, Sr., "Faith's Confession of God's Word," in the *Spirit-Filled Life Bible* (NKJV), Jack W. Hayford, gen. ed. (Nashville, TN: Thomas Nelson Publishers, 1991), p. 1876.

Chapter 5: The Weapon of Praise

1. Jack R. Taylor, *The Hallelujah Factor* (Nashville, TN: Broadman Press, 1983), pp. 31, 33.

Chapter 6: Agreement Brings Boldness

1. Jack Hayford, *Prayer Is Invading the Impossible* (New York: Ballantine Books, 1983), pp. 50-51. Visit Dr. Hayford's website at www.jackhayford.org.
2. Thomas B. White, *The Believer's Guide to Spiritual Warfare* (Ann Arbor, MI: Servant Publications, 1990), p. 155.

Chapter 7: Other Strategies for Battle

1. Arthur Wallis, *God's Chosen Fast: A Spiritual and Practical Guide to Fasting* (Fort Washington, PA: Christian Literature Crusade, 1968), pp. 41-42.
2. Dick Eastman, "Advancing in Spiritual Warfare," in the *Spirit-Filled Life Bible* (NKJV), Jack W. Hayford, gen. ed. (Nashville, TN: Thomas Nelson Publishers, 1991), p. 865.
3. Ibid.

Chapter 8: Assured of Victory

1. R. Arthur Mathews, *Born for Battle: 31 Studies on Spiritual Warfare* (Robesonia, PA: OMF Books, 1978), pp. 26-28.

2. William Gurnall, *The Christian in Complete Armour*, vol. 3, abridged by Ruthanne Garlock, et al. (Carlisle, PA: Banner of Truth Trust, 1989), p. 127.

Chapter 9: Assurance of Salvation
1. T.W. Wilson, quoted in *Topical Encyclopedia of Living Quotations*, Sherwood Wirt and Kersten Beckstrom, eds. (Minneapolis, MN: Bethany House, 1982), p. 11.

Chapter 10: Overcoming Depression and Burnout
1. Archibald D. Hart, *Coping with Depression in the Ministry and Other Helping Professions* (Waco, TX: Word Books, 1984), pp. 4-5.
2. Mrs. Howard Taylor, *Behind the Ranges: Fraser of Lisuland, S. W. China* (London: OMF Books, 1944), pp. 90-91.

Chapter 11: Freedom from Anxiety and Fear
1. Richard K. Avery and Donald S. March, "Every Morning Is Easter Morning," copyright © 1972 by Hope Publishing Co., Carol Stream, IL 60188. All rights reserved. Used by permission.
2. D. James Kennedy, *Turn It to Gold* (Ann Arbor, MI: Servant Publications, 1991), pp. 83-84.

Chapter 12: Freedom from Guilt
1. Diane Mandt Langberg, *Feeling Good, Feeling Bad* (Ann Arbor, MI: Servant Publications, 1991), pp. 192-93.
2. Edwin Louis Cole, *Maximized Manhood: A Guide to Family Survival* (Springdale, PA: Whitaker House, 1982), pp. 118, 120.

Chapter 13: Overcoming Grief and Disappointment
1. Alfred Ells, *One-Way Relationships: When You Love Them More Than They Love You* (Nashville, TN: Thomas Nelson, 1990), p. 114.
2. H. Dale Wright, "Grief in Dysfunctional Families," (seminar presentation at Midwestern Baptist Theological Seminary, Kansas City, Missouri, April 28, 1988).
3. Ells, *One-Way Relationships*, pp. 124-25.

Chapter 14: Regaining Self-Esteem
1. Diane Mandt Langberg, *Feeling Good, Feeling Bad* (Ann Arbor, MI: Servant Publications, 1991), p. 152.

Chapter 15: Warfare for Your Marriage and Broken Relationships
1. Archibald D. Hart, *Healing Life's Hidden Addictions: Overcoming the Closet Compulsions That Waste Your Time and Control Your Life* (Ann Arbor, MI: Servant Publications, 1990), p. 164.
2. Quin Sherrer and Ruthanne Garlock, *How to Pray for Your Family and Friends* (Ann Arbor, MI: Servant Publications, 1990), p. 52.

Chapter 17: Standing Against Childlessness or Abortion
1. "Human Life and Bioethics," *The Family Research Council*, 2009. http://www.frc.org/life—bioethics#abortion (accessed March 17, 2009).
2. Keith Moore and T.V.N. Persaud, *The Developing Human: Clinically Oriented Embryology*, 6th ed. (Philadelphia: W.B. Saunders Co. 1998), pp. 77, 350.
3. Marjorie A. England, *Life Before Birth*, 2nd ed. (London: Mosby-Wolfe, 1996).
4. "Research on Post-Abortion Issues," *AfterAbortion.org*, 1997-2009. http://www.afterabortion.org/reasmor.html (accessed on March 17, 2009). This website is sponsored by the Elliot Institute, P.O. Box 73478, Springfield, IL 62791.

Chapter 18: Victorious and Single
1. Michael Cavanaugh, *God's Call to the Single Adult* (Springdale, PA: Whitaker House, 1986), p. 81.
2. Michael Cavanaugh, founder of Mobilized to Serve, "You Are Complete in Him" (lecture to the student body at Christ for the Nations Institute, Dallas, Texas, March 30,

1992). (To contact this ministry, write: Mobilized to Serve, Elim Fellowship, 7245 College Street, Lima, NY 14485.)

3. Archibald D. Hart, *Healing Adult Children of Divorce: Taking Care of Unfinished Business So You Can Be Whole Again* (Ann Arbor, MI: Servant Publications, 1991), pp. 179-180.

Chapter 19: Material Provision

1. E. W. Bullinger, *The Companion Bible-KJV* (Grand Rapids, MI: Zondervan Bible Publishers, 1964), app., p. 170.1.
2. Harold Lindsell, *Lindsell Study Bible: The Living Bible Paraphrased* (Wheaton, IL: Tyndale House, 1980), p. 1052.

Chapter 20: Protection and Security

1. Thomas B. White, *The Believer's Guide to Spiritual Warfare* (Ann Arbor, MI: Servant Publications, 1990), p. 105.

Chapter 21: Healing

1. Dean Sherman, *Spiritual Warfare for Every Christian: How to Live in Victory and Retake the Land* (Seattle, WA: Frontline Communications, 1990), pp. 147-48.
2. Quin Sherrer and Ruthanne Garlock, *Lord, I Need Your Healing Power: Securing God's Help in Sickness and Trials* (Lake Mary, FL: Charisma Books, 2006), p. 101.
3. Ibid., 105.

Chapter 22: Deliverance

1. E. M. Bounds, *Winning the Invisible War* (Springdale, PA: Whitaker House, 1984), p. 33.
2. Quin Sherrer and Ruthanne Garlock, *Lord, Help Me Break This Habit: You Can Be Free from Doing the Things You Hate* (Grand Rapids, MI: Chosen Books, 2009), pp. 103-104.
3. Ibid.
4. Dean Sherman, *Spiritual Warfare for Every Christian: How to Live in Victory and Retake the Land* (Seattle, WA: Frontline Communications, 1990), p. 85.
5. Neil T. Anderson, *The Bondage Breaker: Overcoming Negative Thoughts, Irrational Feelings, Habitual Sins,* 2nd ed. (Eugene, OR: Harvest House Publishers, 2000), pp. 258-259.

Chapter 23: Intercession for Others

1. Joy Dawson, in the *New Spirit-Filled Life Bible* (NKJV), Jack Hayford, gen. ed. (Nashville, TN: Thomas Nelson Publishers, 2002), p. 1078.
2. James Strong, *Strong's Exhaustive Concordance of the Bible* (Grand Rapids, MI: Zondervan, 2001), Hebrew reference #6293.
3. Dick Eastman, "Advancing in Spiritual Warfare," in the *Spirit-Filled Life Bible* (NKJV), Jack W. Hayford, gen. ed. (Nashville, TN: Thomas Nelson Publishers, 1991), p. 1108.
4. Dutch Sheets, *Intercessory Prayer: How God Can Use Your Prayers to Move Heaven and Earth* (Ventura, CA: Regal, 1996), p. 170.
5. Ibid., pp. 208-209.
6. Judson Cornwall, *Praying the Scriptures: Communicating with God in His Own Words* (Lake Mary, FL: Creation House, 1990), pp. 212-13.

Chapter 24: Battling Against Deception

1. *The E.W. Bullinger Companion Bible* (Grand Rapids, MI: Zondervan, 1964), appendix 19, 25.

Chapter 26: Praying for Spiritual Leaders

1. William Gurnall, *The Christian in Complete Armour,* vol. 1, abridged by Ruthanne Garlock, et al. (Carlisle, PA: Banner of Truth Trust, 1986), p. 84.
2. C. Peter Wagner, *Prayer Shield: How to Intercede for Pastors, Christian Leaders, and Others on the Spiritual Frontlines* (Ventura, CA: Regal Books, 1992), p. 50 (reference from the manuscript version). Used with permission of Dr. Wagner.

3. Joy Dawson, *Intercession, Thrilling and Fulfilling* (Seattle, WA: YWAM Publishing, 1997), pp. 101-102.
4. Cindy Jacobs, *Possessing the Gates of the Enemy* (Tarrytown, NY: Chosen Books, 1991), pp. 126-28.
5. Terry Tekyl, *Preyed On or Prayed For* (Muncie, IN: Prayer Point Press, 2000), p. 136. Visit Dr. Tekyl's website at www.renewalministries.com.

Chapter 27: Mobilizing Prayer Groups
1. Jamie Buckingham, *The Nazarene: Intimate Insights into the Savior's Life* (Ann Arbor, MI: Servant Publications, 1991), pp. 87-89.
2. A good source of information for setting up your church's intercessory prayer group is found in *The Power of Church Intercession*, a pamphlet published by Breakthrough, Inc., P.O. Box 121, Lincoln, VA 20160, www.intercessors.org/publications.

Chapter 28: Praying for Your Neighborhood, City and Nation
1. Steve Hawthorne and Graham Kendrick, *Prayerwalking: Praying On-Site with Insight* (Orlando, FL: Creation House, 1993), pp. 15-17. Visit Steve Hawthorne's website at www.waymakers.org.
2. Alvin VanderGriend, *Intercessors for America* Newsletter, March 1999. Visit the HOPE (Houses of Prayer Everywhere) Ministries website at www.hopeministries.org.
3. Ibid.
4. John Dawson, *Taking Our Cities for God: How to Break Spiritual Strongholds* (Lake Mary, FL: Creation House, 1989), pp. 115-16.

BOOKS BY QUIN SHERRER AND RUTHANNE GARLOCK

Lord, Help Me Break This Habit

Lord, I Need to Pray with Power

Lord, I Need Your Healing Power

Grandma, I Need Your Prayers

The Beginners Guide to Receiving the Holy Spirit

Becoming A Spirit-Led Mom

God Be with Us: A Daily Guide to Praying for Our Nation

Prayer Partnerships

Praying Prodigals Home

The Making of a Spiritual Warrior

Prayers Women Pray

How to Pray for Your Children (revised edition)

A Woman's Guide to Getting Through Tough Times

A Woman's Guide to Spirit-filled Living

A Woman's Guide to Breaking Bondages

The Spiritual Warrior's Prayer Guide

A Woman's Guide to Spiritual Warfare

How to Pray for Family and Friends

How to Forgive Your Children

BOOKS BY QUIN SHERRER

Prayers from A Grandmother's Heart

Miracles Happen When You Pray

Listen, God Is Speaking to You

The Warm and Welcome Home

Good Night, Lord

A House of Many Blessings (with Laura Watson)

How to Pray for Your Children

BOOKS BY RUTHANNE GARLOCK

Before We Kill and Eat You (the story of H.B. Garlock)

Fire in His Bones

You may contact the authors through their respective websites:

Quin: www.quinsherrer.com

Ruthanne: www.garlockministries.org

OTHER BOOKS BY QUIN SHERRER & RUTHANNE GARLOCK

THE BEGINNER'S GUIDE TO
RECEIVING THE HOLY SPIRIT
ISBN 978-08307-3393-4

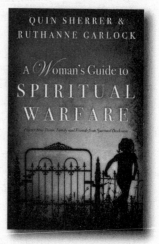

A WOMAN'S GUIDE TO
SPIRITUAL WARFARE
ISBN 978-08307-4748-1

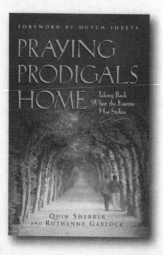

PRAYING PRODIGALS HOME
ISBN 978-08307-2563-2

Available at Bookstores Everywhere!

Visit www.regalbooks.com to join Regal's FREE e-newsletter. You'll get useful excerpts from our newest releases and special access to online chats with your favorite authors. Sign up today!

This powerful prayer guide encourages "giant-slaying" faith without abandoning sound biblical principles. Each chapter compelled me into audacious prayer, which not only changed my circumstances but also my perception of God and His extravagant response to my requests. Thank you for writing this dynamic book.

MARY GLAZIER
President, Windwalkers International
Anchorage, Alaska

Throughout my years of teaching spiritual warfare in Aglow and in churches, the books by Quin and Ruthanne have been an invaluable resource. *The Spiritual Warrior's Prayer Guide* is especially strategic in empowering both women and men to employ the tools Christ gives believers to win spiritual battles. Biblically sound, clearly and practically presented, it is a powerful weapon in a Christian's arsenal. I have taught from it for a long time and will continue to do so.

MARILYN REJ
Aglow Southeast Regional Leader
Columbia, South Carolina

Everybody at one point or another in his or her life needs a breakthrough. A crisis is not the time to be searching the house for a key. Quin Sherrer and Ruthanne Garlock show us how to be prepared before we need it.

MARK RUTLAND, PH.D.
President, Oral Roberts University

This book is the finest toolbox for effective spiritual warfare that I have seen.

DR. C. PETER WAGNER
Author and Chancellor, Wagner Leadership Institute
Colorado Springs, Colorado

PRAISE FOR

THE SPIRITUAL WARRIOR'S PRAYER GUIDE

My longtime friends, Quin and Ruthanne, supply here practical guidelines for equipping intercessors to become more strategic and effective in using God's Word in spiritual warfare. The arsenal of Scripture, divided by numerous topics, provides the reader with the most pertinent verses to pray in a given situation. *The Spiritual Warrior's Prayer Guide* is a valuable resource for every intercessor's library.

ELIZABETH ALVES
Bestselling Author of *Becoming a Prayer Warrior,* Bulverde, Texas

The Spiritual Warrior's Prayer Guide is as well named as it is well written. Every Christian prayer warrior will want to have this book to carry along with their Bible. It is for the new Christian as well as the mature one. You will find it easy to use and direct to the point. I am the Chairman of the Heartland Apostolic Prayer Network (HAPN) with leaders and networks in 35 states, and I recommend this guide to all of them. Do yourself and your loved ones a big favor and learn to pray the prayers in this wonderful book!

DR. JOHN BENEFIEL
Senior Pastor, Church on the Rock, Oklahoma City, Oklahoma

This book is a source of knowledge, good judgment and wisdom for those who desire to pray effectively. Quin Sherrer and Ruthanne Garlock share the proven insights they have gained through precept and practice.

GERMAINE COPELAND
Bestselling Author of *Prayers That Avail Much* (Family Book Series)
Monroe, Georgia